I0488333

Circles Sacred

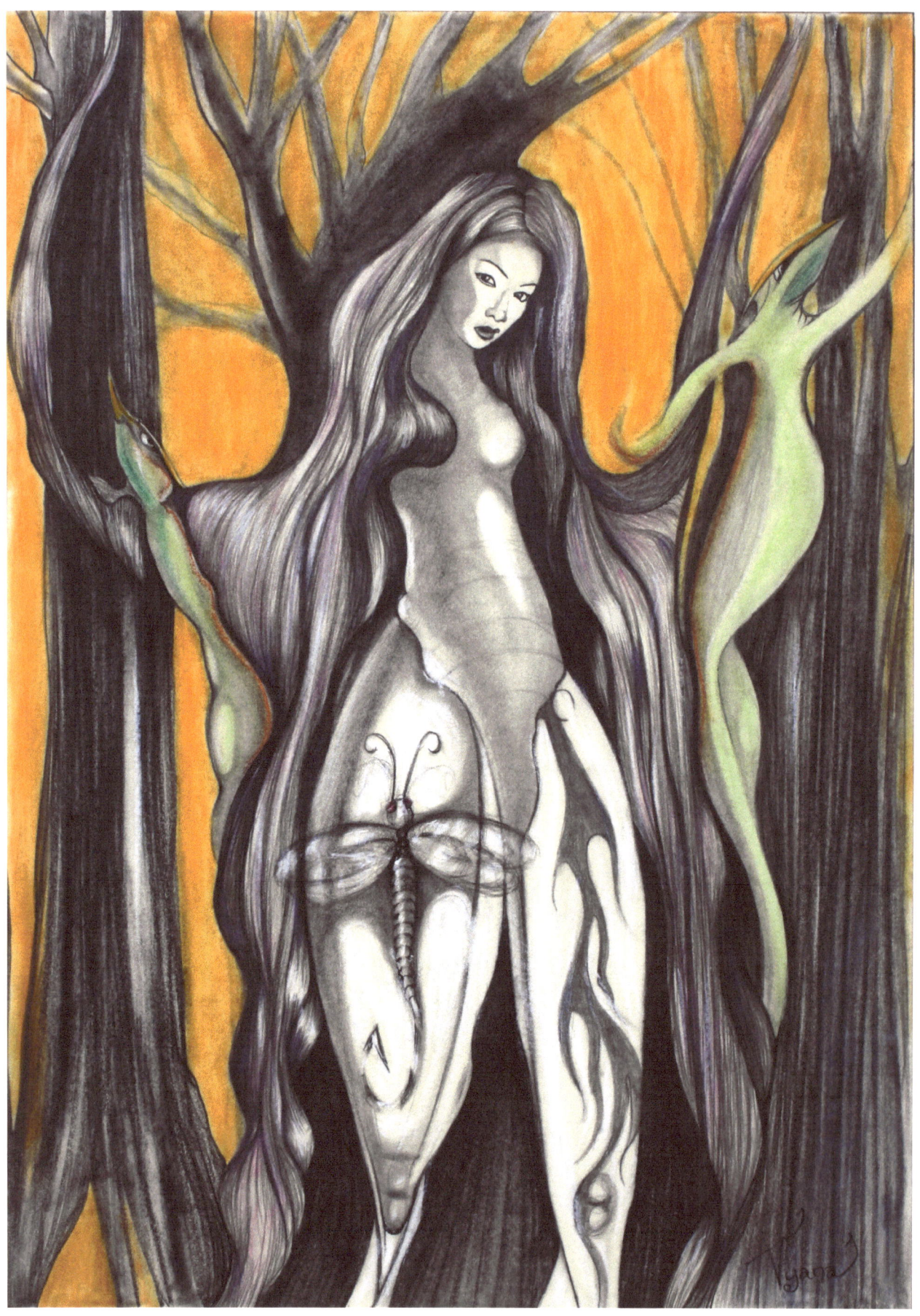

Circles Sacred

FOREVER IS AS NEAR AS YOUR HEART

Vyana Slattery

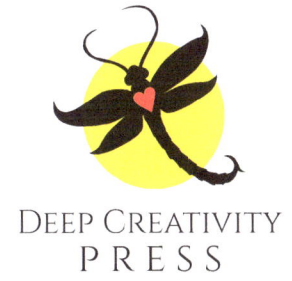

DEEP CREATIVITY
PRESS

Copyright © 2017 by Vyana M. Slattery
All rights reserved. This book or any portion thereof
may not be reproduced or used in any manner whatsoever
without the express written permission of the publisher
except for the use of brief quotations in a book review.

Printed in the United States of America

First Printing, 2017

ISBN 978-0-9994158-0-1

Deep Creativity Press
PO Box 2652
Grand Rapids MI 49501

www.DeepCreativity.org

book design by Devin DuMond
Hatch Creative Services, LLC
www.hatchgr.com

Dedicated to
my loving parents, William and Phyllis Slattery
my children, dearly beloved
my close friends and allies
my students

to Devin DuMond, who designed this beautiful book to
be experienced by others, for her aesthetic brilliance, and
manifesting the instincts of her father in Circles Sacred.

Endless blessings to our ancestors.

Peace and calm,
vyana

Mourning Star

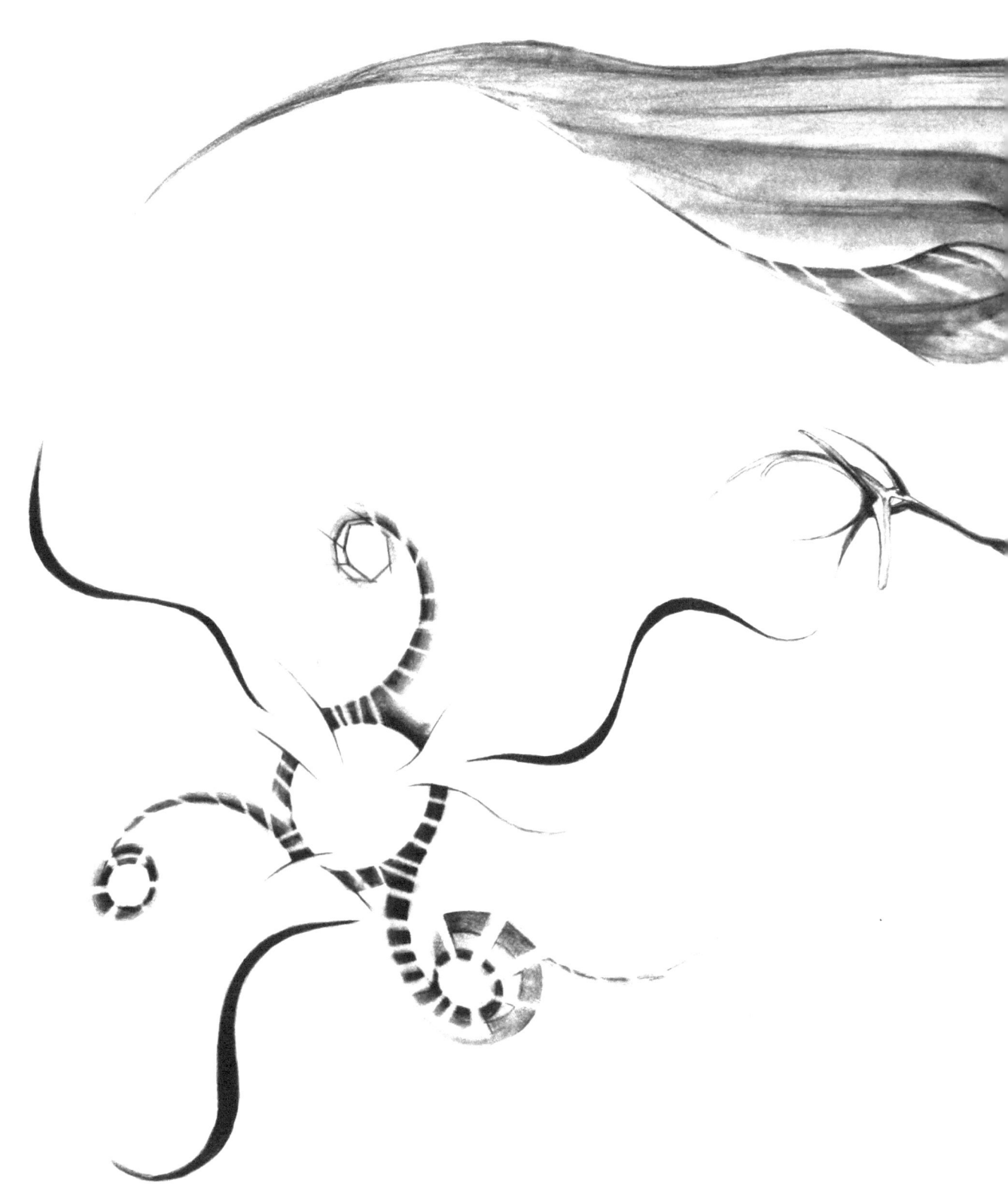

Life begins with mourning

Every new beginning is about

giving something up

losing something

indeed, something dies!

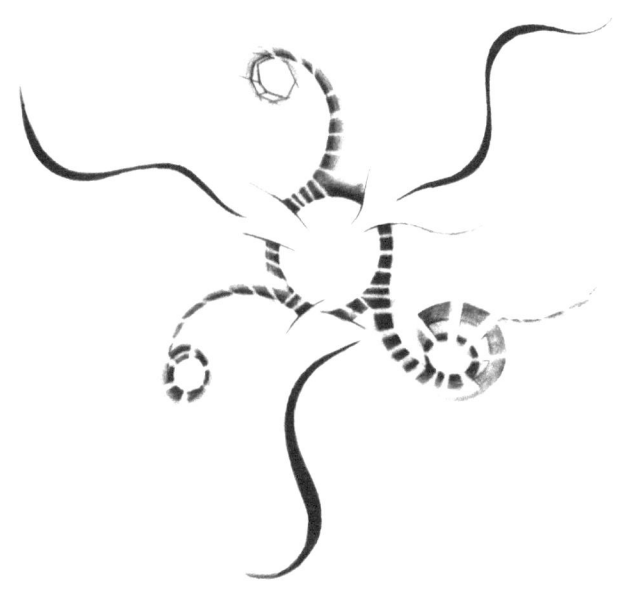

Life begins with mourning.

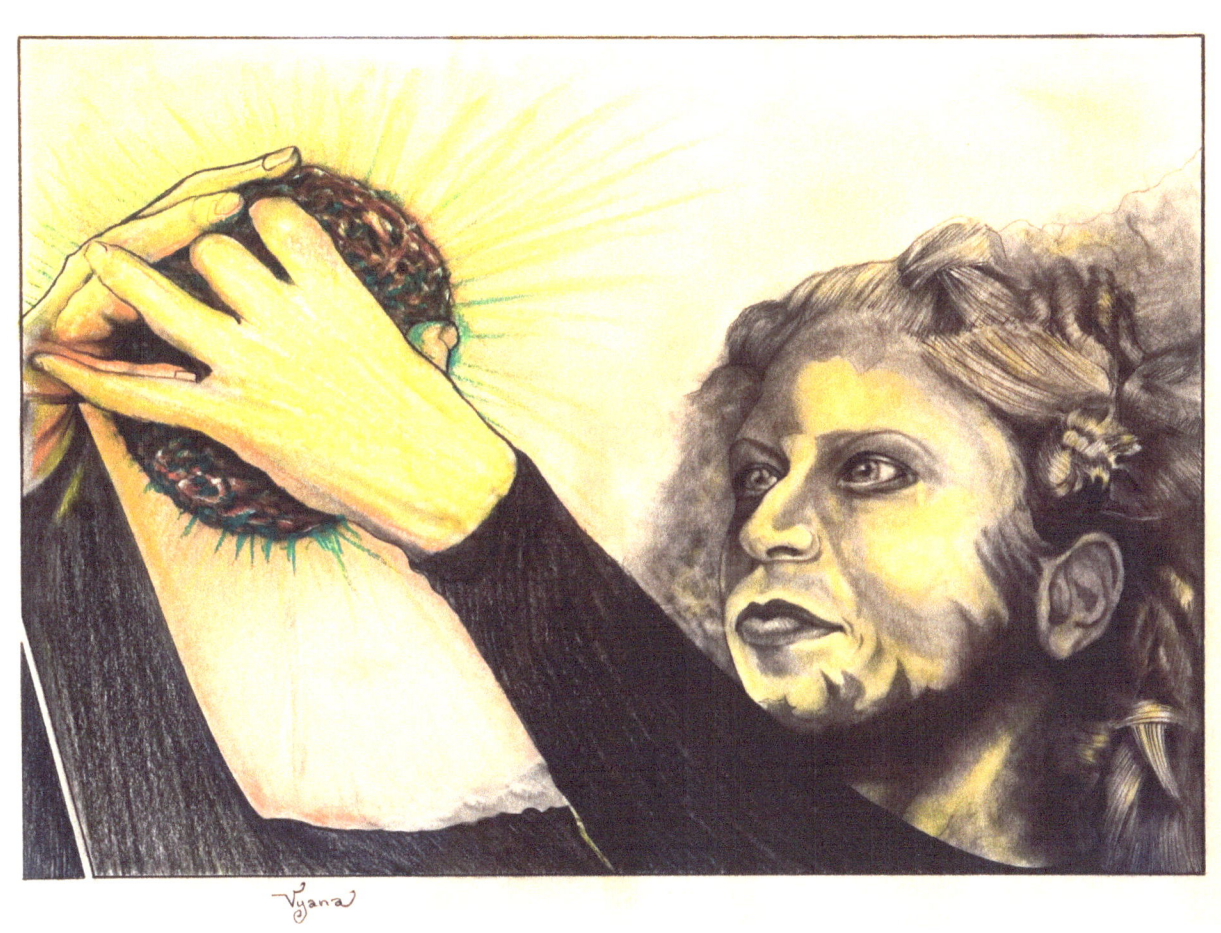

Unfolding cycles, ever nourishing an aesthetic
sense of natural beauty in mOtherUniverse
expressing herself as lovingKindness.

Contents

INTRODUCTION

I love words

— Angel Madhuri, *Pune, India*
    student of vyana
    poet, mathematician, and computer scientist

1.
... practicing ...
I was waiting for this healing to happen
and, I am feeling better.
... talking through the mail,
it is as if I am talking to you really.
It is fun, love is beautiful.

And the Death card mirrors me too.
I have experienced that dying too in living...
This is not easy, but everyone
has their own challenges

I see more and more light
after the darkness overwhelms
I see more and more light
after the darkness is lessening.

2.
I see power after the hours
of being powerless.
Struggling... struggling... then smooth.
In all of my years I never
experienced not pain.
Every second was as if a century.
I had nothing in place, neither
mind, body, or silence.
These experiences drained me
and dragged me.
It was as if it were never
going to end and I will admit it.

3.
But it was a lie... I became very impatient...
Everything was in the proper place.
I saw everyone for help, but
no one had a solution to my problem.
No one knew what I was going through...
No life at all.
Empty. Nothing. Scared. Terrified. Afraid.
Hope.
But now tears of joy...
I am out!
I have come out of the dead.

4.
Thank you so much for being here for me.
I needed someone to talk to me endlessly and...
Give me those words that
my ears want to listen to and hear.
I love words.

feather

— Madhuri, *Pune, India*
 student of vyana
 poet, mathematician, and computer scientist

Fear has made me the person i am today.
I see it whenever something new comes,
for there is a fear of change,
which always seems to be the same.

It comes to change me so that i have no option
other than to move, or die fearing.

There was real solid fear in my life that trapped me,
but after it had been mastered
it is a feather.

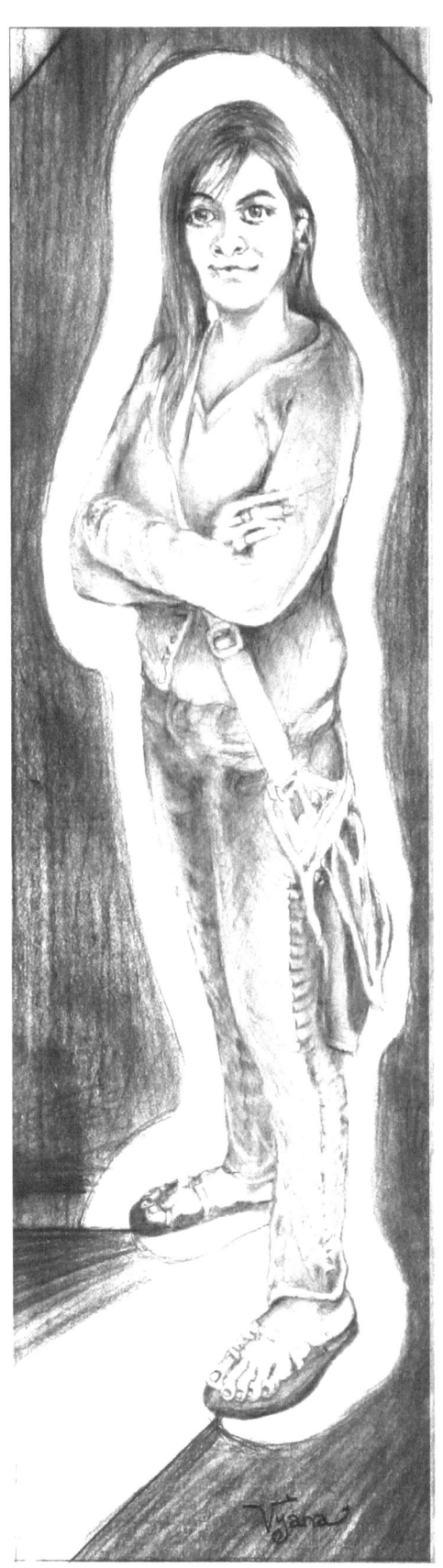

Forward

— Jane Gallimore, *London, England*
  Professor, Animal Activist, Energy Healer/Reiki Master

Vyana has a mind at peace with itself = The deep understanding of who we are and why we are here. A knowing that only one who understands the universe—our infinite power—can only know.

He is the wisdom keeper of the Soul. Our Soul, using magic with words and pictures he expresses deep creativity and harmonic resonance. Expanding energy in depth and frequency throughout the pages of this beautifully illustrated book of poems. This is truly a case of ancient wisdom being new again. This demonstrates the law of resonance with life force energy through the medium of the artist and his creativity through conscious choices and heart-centred works. This is a space to linger, enjoy and expand ever deeper into Circles Sacred.

Preface

Circles Sacred is book like a journey without a map that has no end-destination, but is of spirals and openings, of meanderings and closings, and of lingering pauses. I traveled the world and words, phrases, and images arrived with little effort on my part. I merely had to observe, listen keenly, and have an open heart as the endless series of synchronicities were experienced within each moment.

The apparently solitary journey I am sharing with you is one where I met new friends, and loving allies, as we shared our experiences that deepened and expanded our awareness by participating in the vagaries and mysteries within livinglovingliving. And, it did not take long to realize this journey, both personal and impersonal, was one in which I was not alone at all, but I was being fully enveloped, entrained in, and embraced by so many fellow travelers. Life became a wandering through flowering gardens of endless tonal variations, myriad shapes, thought-forms, and hues.

My travels revealed so much, just like an onion and it's multiple layers of realities, or like weather reports with their endless fluctuations, or in my meditation practices opening further perceptions. My realities became conjoined as the impulses of living nomadically propelled me on and on in endless delight.

As I was being challenged or embraced, something was always being expressed, and beauty became empathy as I surrendered to these precious and sanctified states of communion with all and everything: Circles Sacred.

... slowing down ...

... step-by-step ...

... heart2heart...

... in lovingKindness ...

— vyana, News from My Universe and YOU.

PART ONE

Circles Sacred

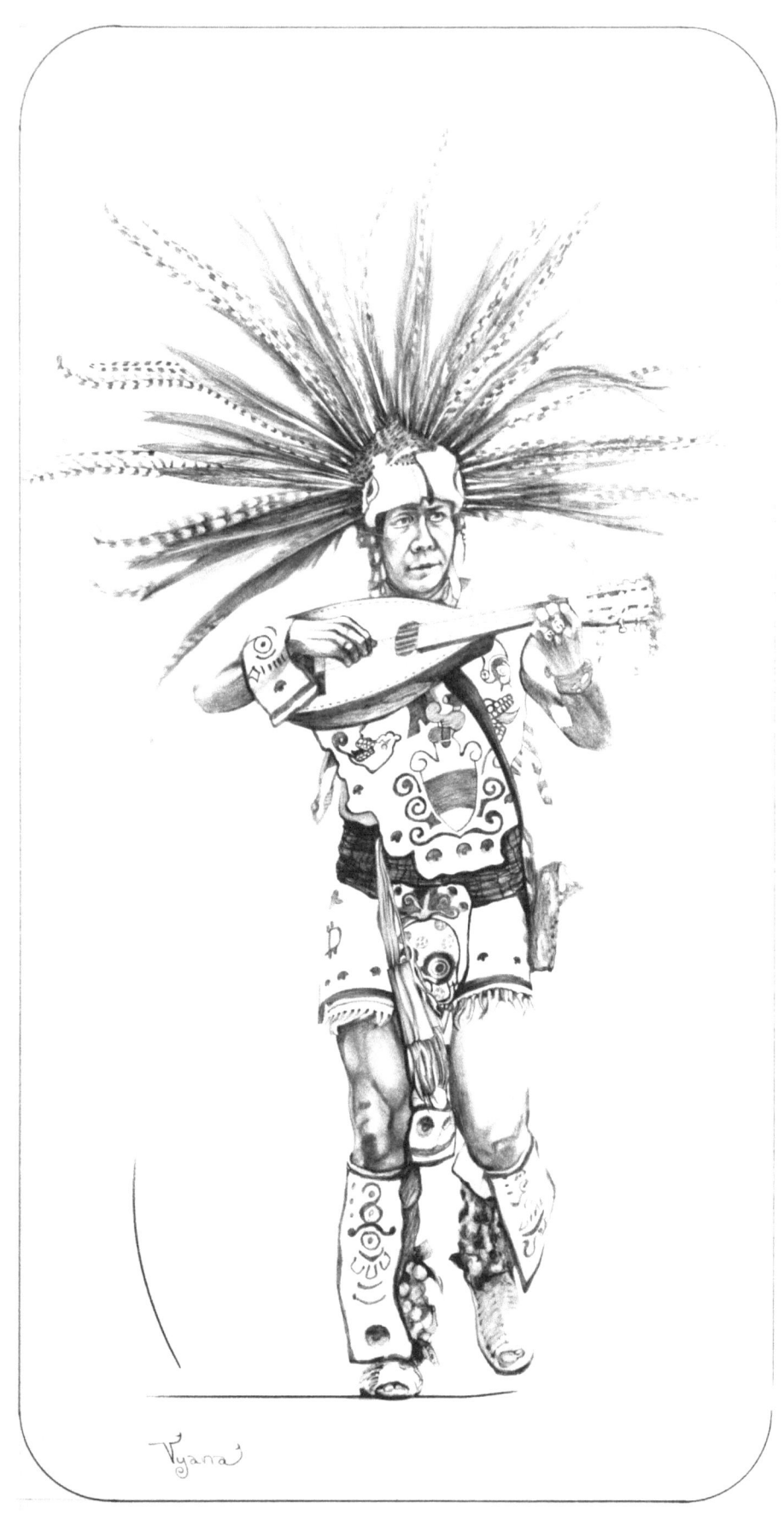

CIRCLESsacred

Contracts signified:

revolution

repeating patterns

no end, no beginning

embodied energies

reconnecting

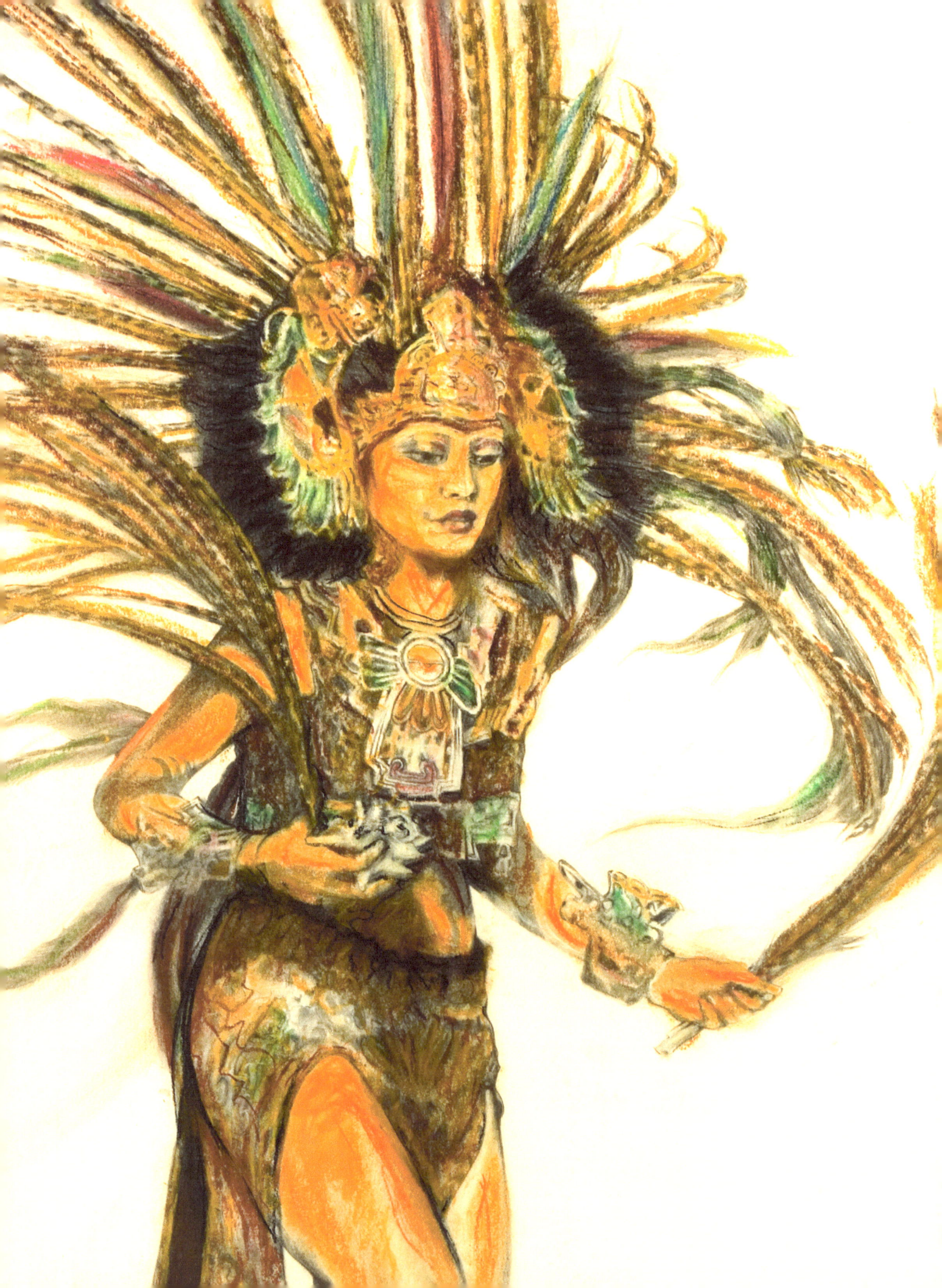

Spirit dancing

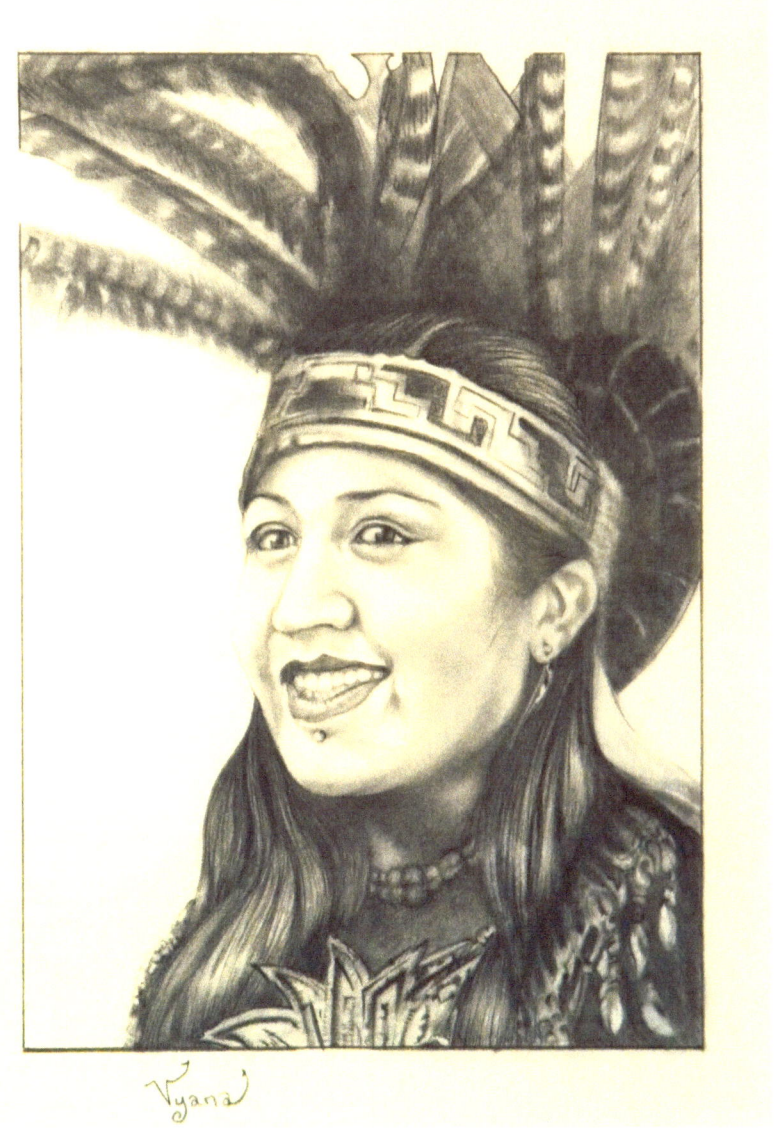

It is not as if we are a spirit,

because it is about being

spirited

and energized.

"fit"

means fitness

to fit uncompromisingly
into your inner and outer
environments

inducing harmony

health

and

kindness

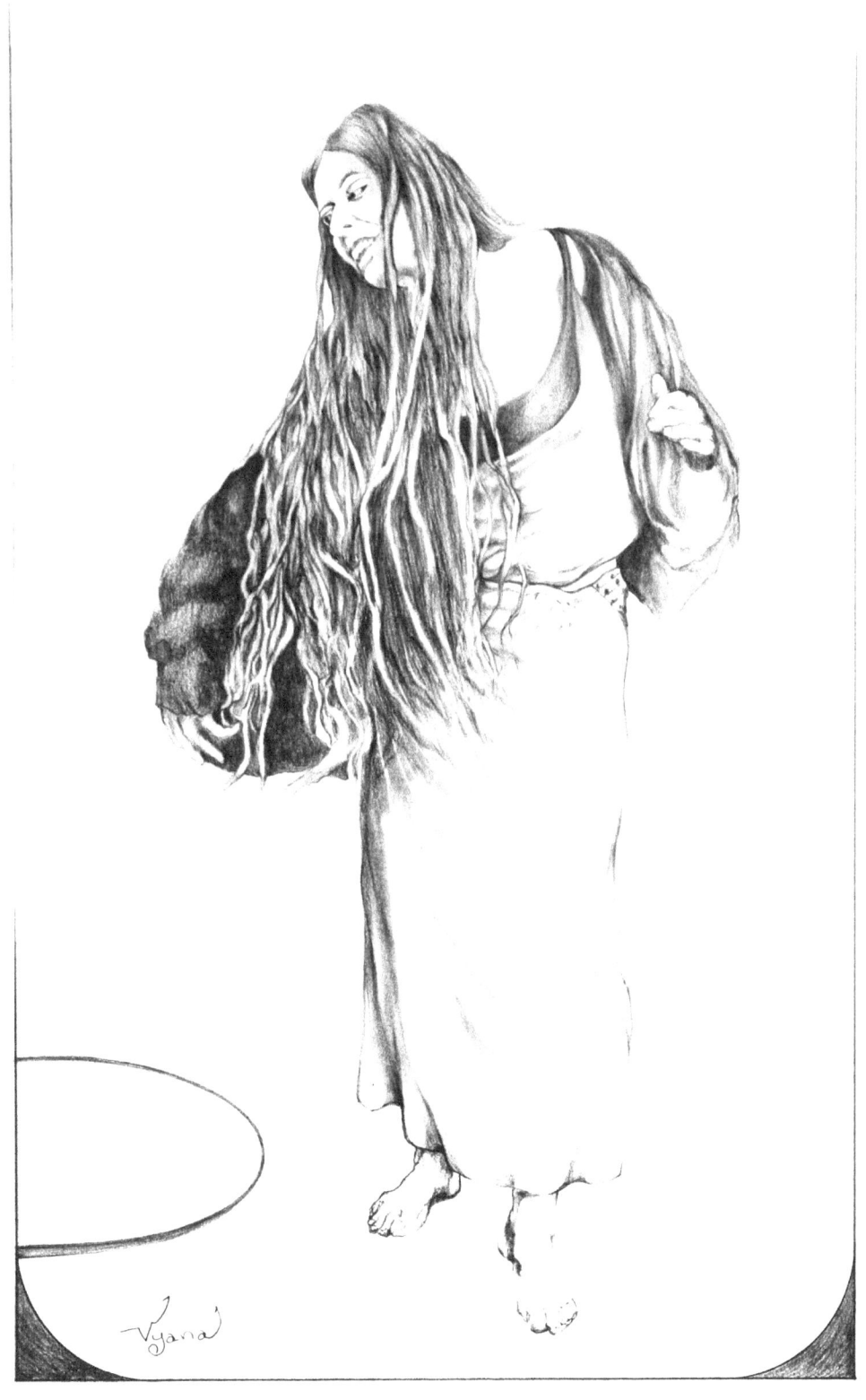

It is in standing stillness that we become observant,
and find that we are nourished on many levels.

Black Ravens/White Ravens

black ravens feminine dark
so-called black
as black absorbs all hues
yet, often streaks with iridescent flutters
white ravens white flames
reflecting all the hues
as active projections into the World
reflections two
the sacred masculine
sensitive
gentle
tender
compassionateStrength
the Mystical Union
2-Spirit
one
of which i am
love is
heart
heart 2 heart
peace
calm
serene
love
is

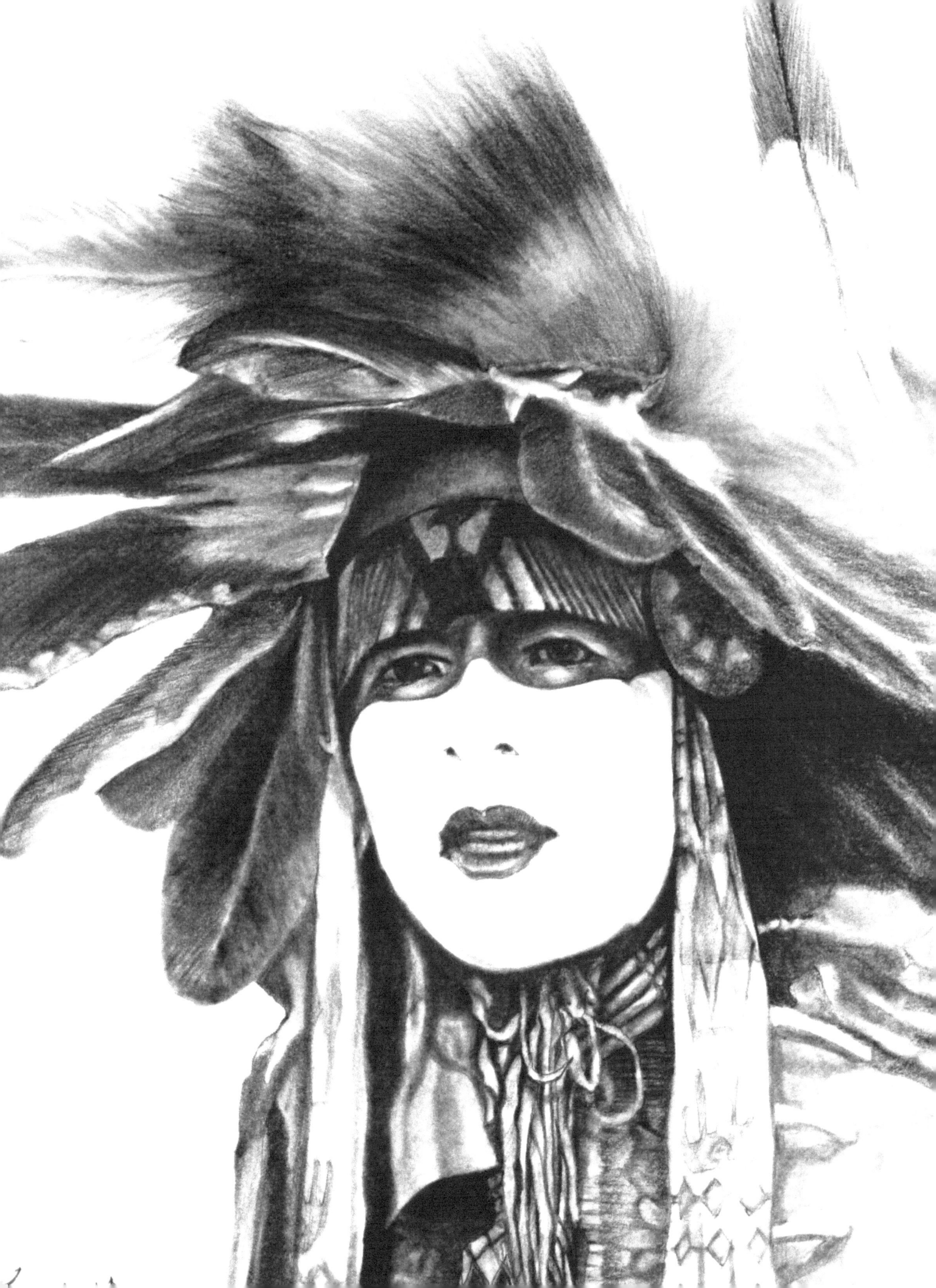

anti-rhythms, out-of-rhythm rhythms, and rhythms

what is hatred of the body?
what is hatred of specific body parts?
what induced these anti-body attitudes?
war-bodies, warring bodies, warrior bodies
manipulating intentions?
antibody medicines inducing more of our anti-body hatreds?
through absorption my sadness returns from
dwelling within hate-filled energy fields
what price do i pay when i hear anti-missiles, and anti-tank weapons?
thus, does this not make war anti-war?
Ummm, this makes sense to someone, eh?
it must be the anti-war war hawks!
so, my sadness imprinted into multi-layered energy fields returns
to the absorption from hate-centered energy fields
we, i/we end up with out-of-rhythm rhythmic hate fields flowing.

2.
my spirit-body begins swaying-dancing at the edge of beyond
and, hesitantly showing itself: "I just want to danceFLOW"
it is movement,
but, i want to stepStop,
but there is no going back
for sadly there will be nothing even to re-mix
but, now, however, it is show time,
for there is no going back,
yet, a what is the matter?
and, a voice speaks twice to me:
"Let it go!"
"Let it go!"
a contrarian voice, it must be speaking of rhythms-to-be.
no more doubting questions will be addressed for sure!

3.
i begin to feel something in the air
and colors layered from etherSpace appear
yet, again, a censoring voice, "What does it matter?"
yet me: "Let go, let go."
so, i shut up!!!!
now feeling ether-air visualizations powerful
dancing into me expanding
dancing into me exploring
dancing into me discovering
I can dance!
I can dance!
truly now, there is no going back
enlivened and in-spirited

COSMIC CURVES:
choreography
atmosphere
creativity
expression
interpretation
time
tempo
phrasing
timing
musicality
rhythmical structures
dynamic
me
spirit dancing
spirit dancing me
meUniverse
Universe
love
love is

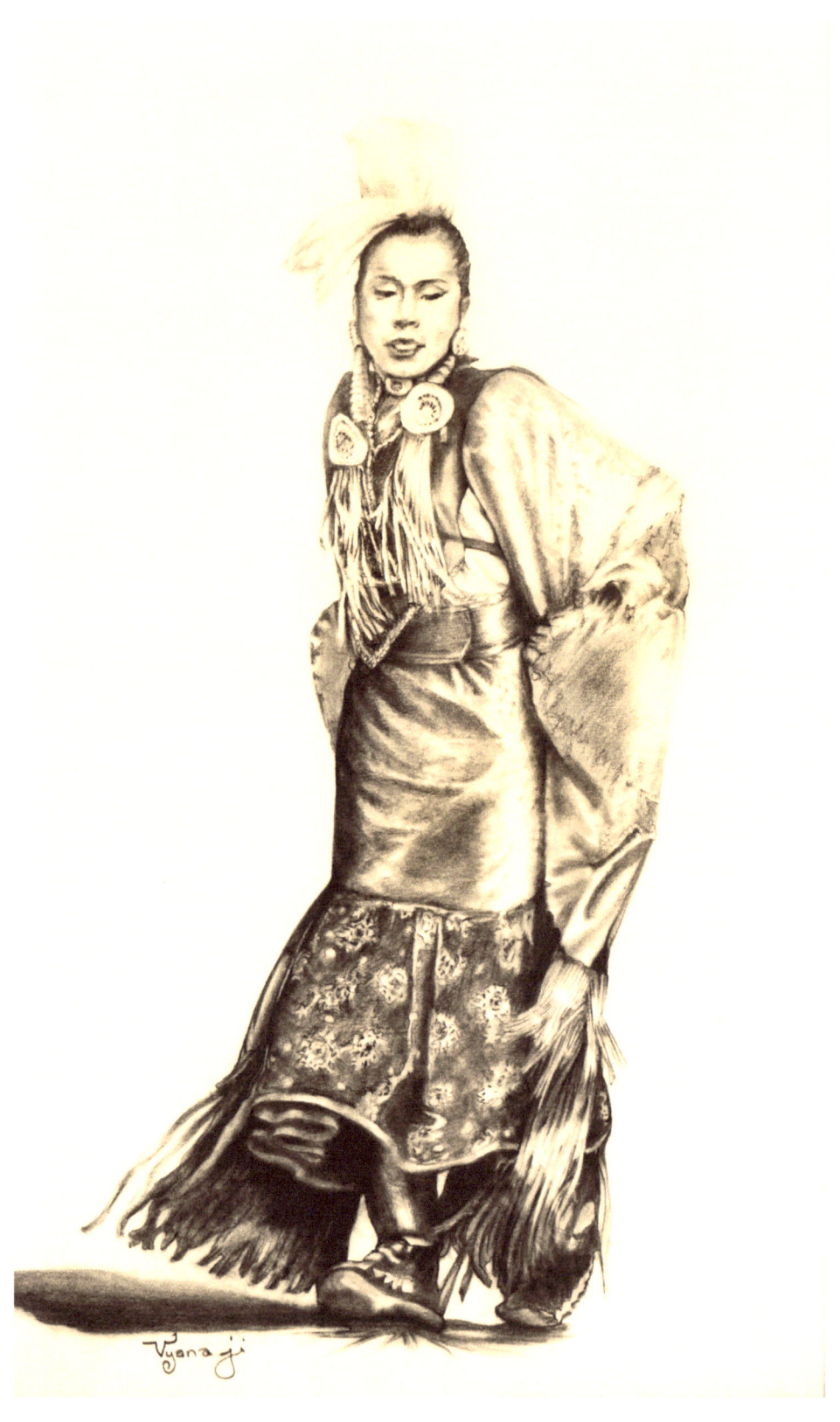

Soul Beautiful

... in livinglovingliving our spirit advances
embodied and connecting with self and all others.

heart's Secret DANCING

looking in touching my heart's secrets

glimpse s of images enchanted

speaking whisperings of passages of tantric secrets

meditating upon genetic codes in matrix crop circles

touching into hollow marrow bones with tendons changing

somatic techniques of

iron shirts integrating subversions into mega shadows

sparking into secrets of emotions dancing

of dancing shadows and emotions dancing

angry women archetypes of feminist paradigms shifting

subversions Workshop integrating

the hollow bones caring of somatic secrets

passages of integrations by dancing Shaolin shamans

caring of heart's secret-E-motions

the dancing whisperings of looking in

Energy Fields: Keep Moving!

The ceaseless convolutions within all energy fields
can be sensed through relaxed alertness.
And, although these are often unpredictable,
and not definable,
they are nonetheless full of wonder and awe
to the quiet observer.

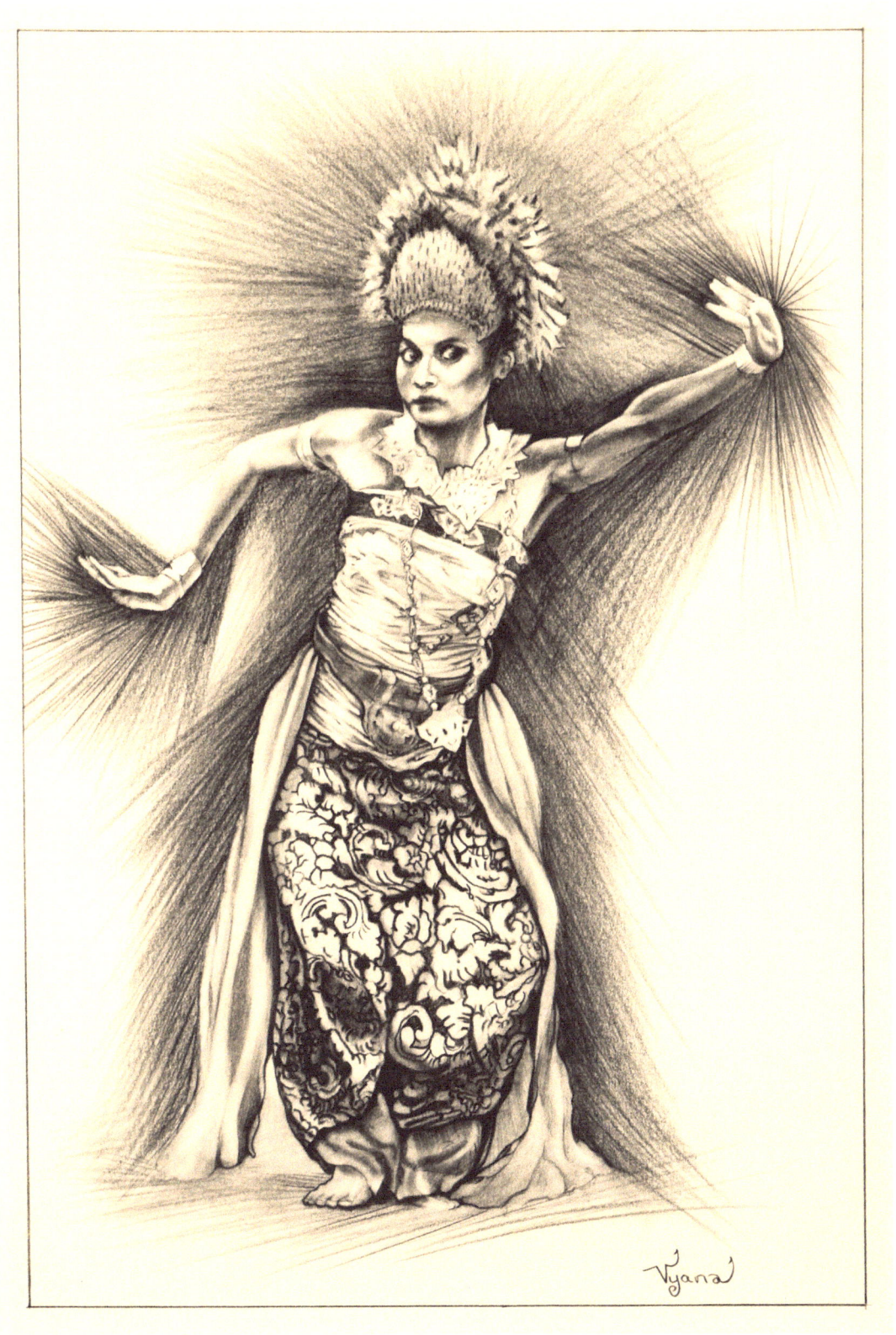

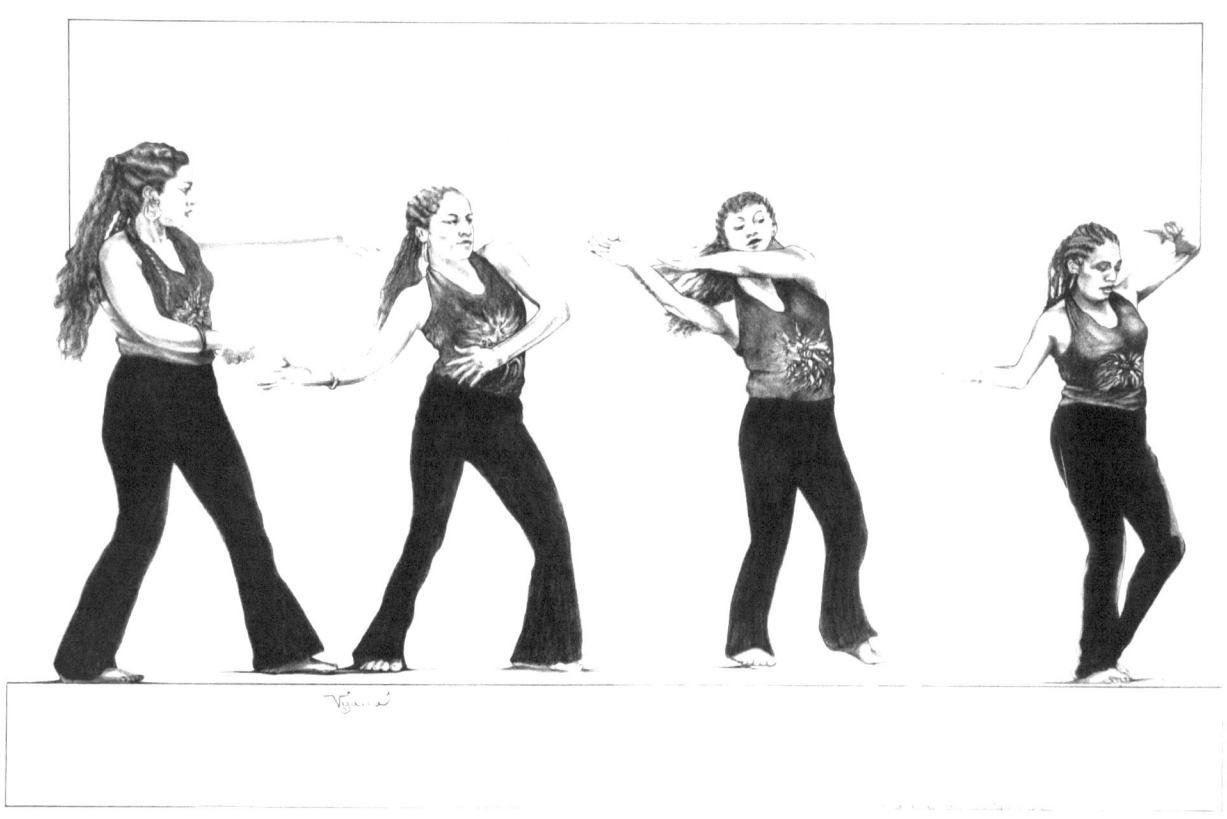

paso doble

1.
ether blue resonances as i extend through the portal from the density of the treed woods,
yellow-green-brown-grey embracing

to unfolding into azure blue pond that i refer to as my lake in a silvery blue sky mirror today i
resonate with it's pristine quiescence and it soothes and i enter

2.
sensing reverberations in sides of my head pulse sounding orange and blue, and blue and orange.
embryo belly emerald green-gold lichen on surfaces of rock observed keenly and softly
feeling weirdGood balanced breathing out and breathing in

3.
giant turtle emerges from black-green depths
with algae stringer streams flowing from it's ancient earthWater shell

flip splash whitish-blue marble droplets exploding everywhere
a fish with it's shining silver-green-blue wetness exposed
attention shifting to swans appearing S-Curved necks beautiful ascended and babies four gliding

16

4.
now on surface of outside skin reverberating to inside surface skin within

a twist, a turn, sensing the s-l-o-w turning of my head re-focusing below
breathing within
breath within
within

a calling voice, an embryo within the basin of my seaWomb
sanctified space

5.
the blue-black fishes below hither and slither slowly today at 1/2 speed

i observe and i wonder contradictory me

sinking eyes observing deeper and deeper now disappeared

a figure emerges, giant turtle again blackish granulated brown textures ancient
with ivory white claws as big as my feet but thicker more power-full

oh, no, turtle quickens submerging now!

6.
silvery tendons stretching long and twisting as i sense me moving

feeling pulsing red heart blood so slowly
rhythmically beckoning
a quieting
a solemnity
a contenting spirit
and, all of me

slow, slow below within a
yellow incandescent
glow softening
setting
settling
into
soothing
ever
so soothing
&
done

Intonations

1.
turquoise ocean eyes penetrating the nature of me
she sea dragons licking salty rocks
flying fish eating stars

it is strange how much i adore those words
writing and listening
just words coming and going
just words here and there
just words with intonations of soul
just words

How can this be?
words dismantle me
dislocate and transfigure the linear me
words pitifully unfeeling
can decapitate me
can break my heart

2.
traffic noisy rushing by
messing with my spirit projecting
the randomness of my intentions,
and the intentions of other minds as well

truth so difficult, so challenging me.
i am suspended upside down from a tree
unable to write of scenarios new

3.
a familiar strange phenomenon urges me,
and itches at my soul

4.
i begin to write anew
and this makes no sense to me
i begin to write
words i love
words from my soul
silly words, any words,
they embrace me so
i write
i write
i write
i write

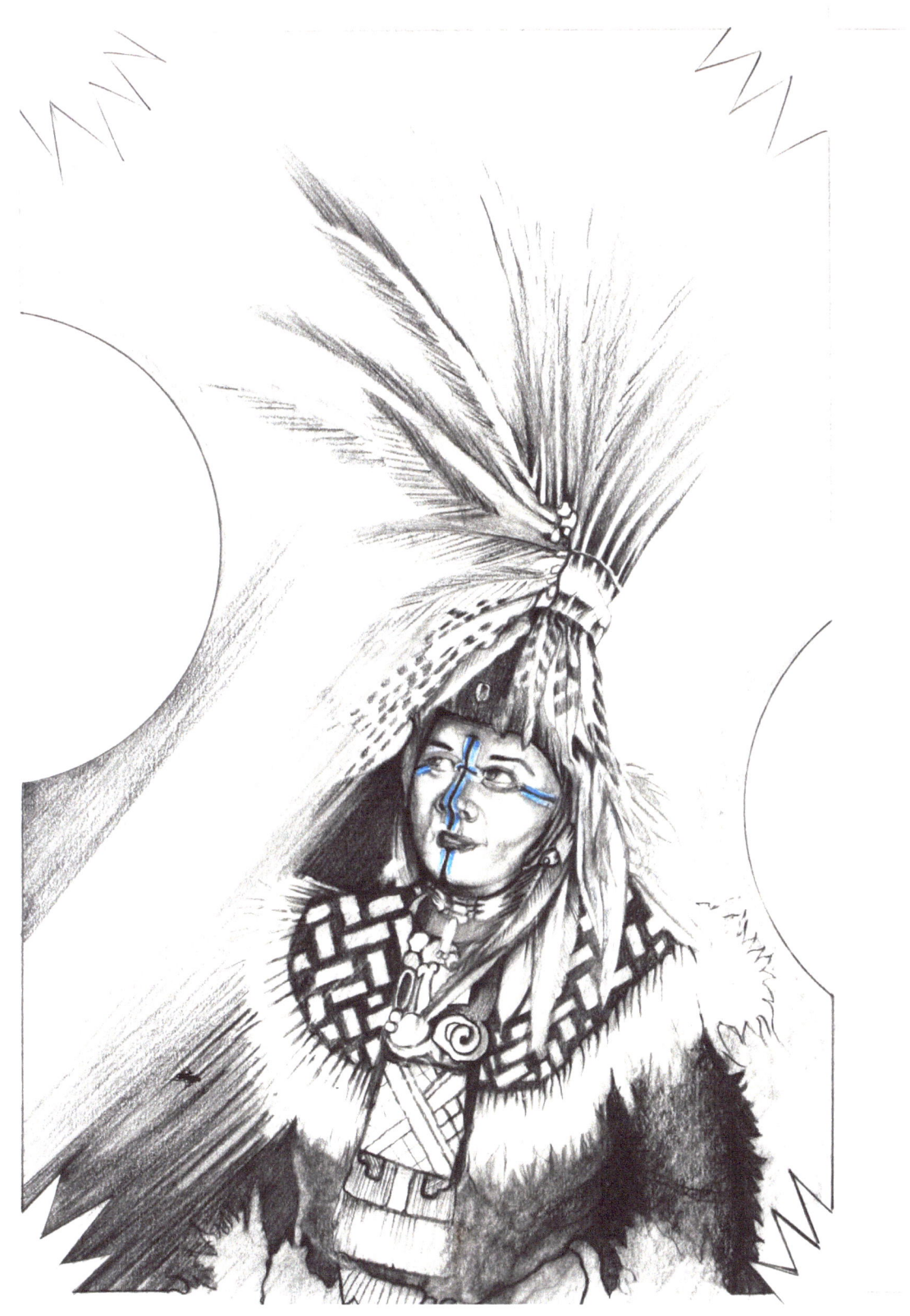

Mirror of the soul

Conscious evolution is determined by our
degree of attachment to gravity.

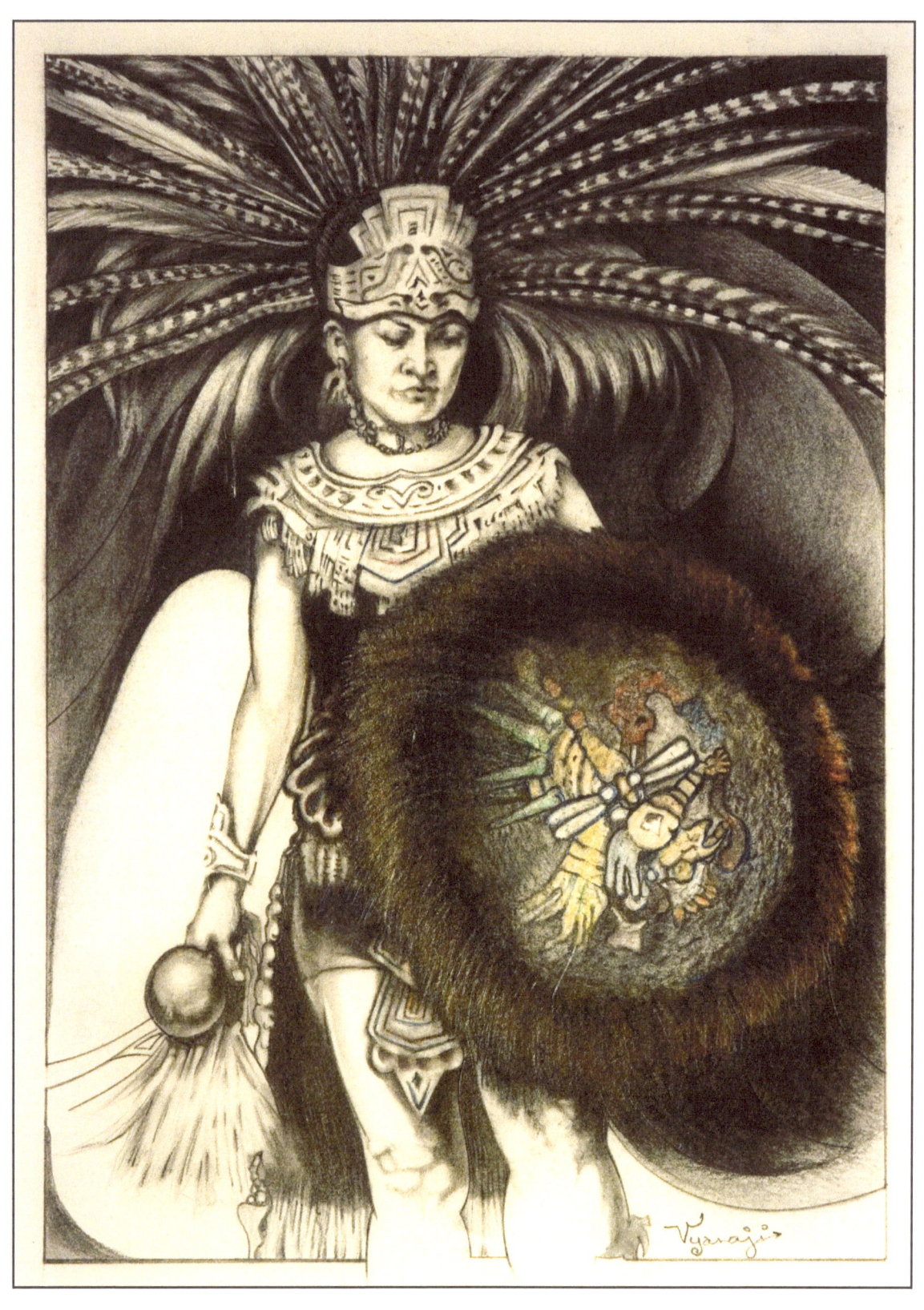

Spirit dancing

peace from within
loving-energies-in-motion

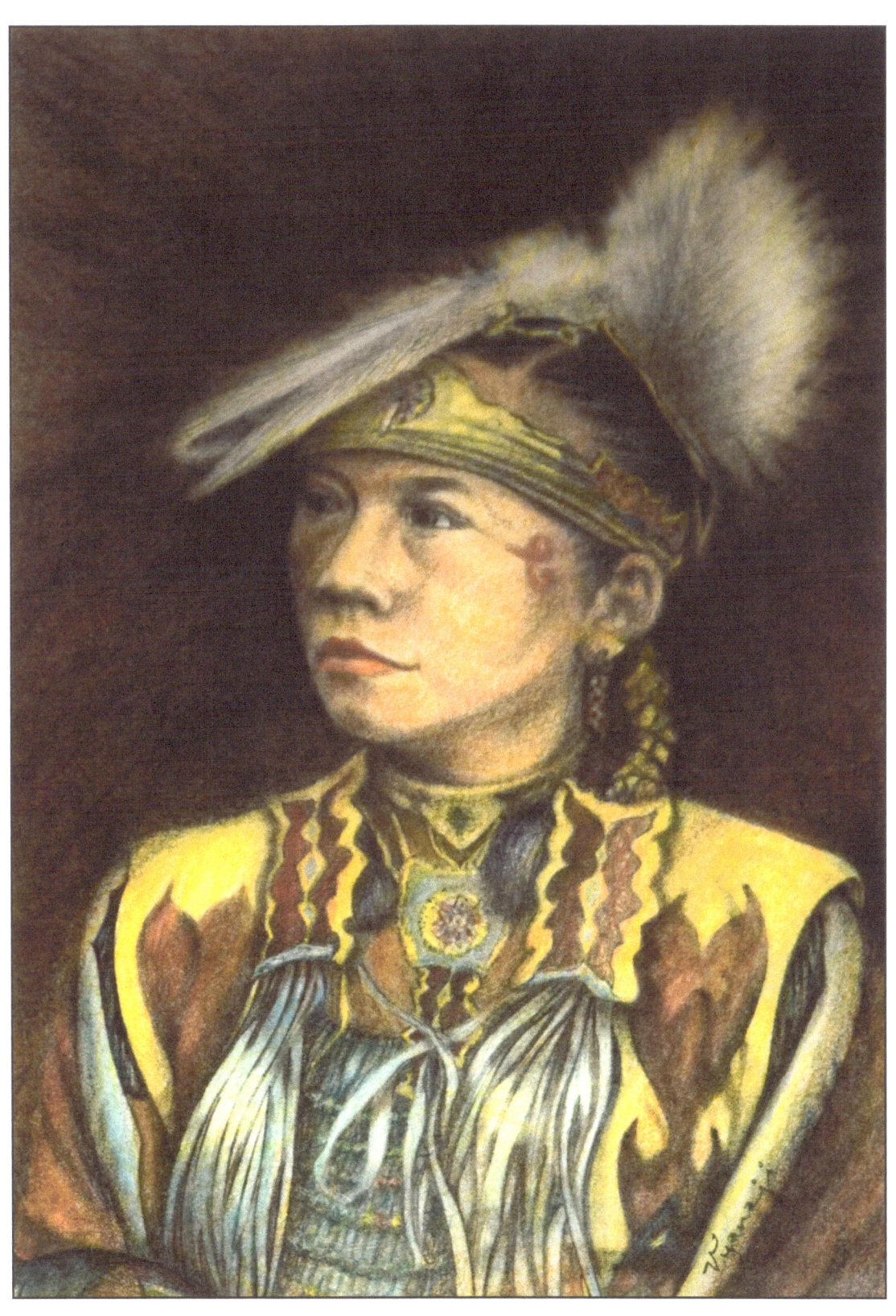

expanding and deepening connectedness ...
mitakuye oyasin – "all my relations."

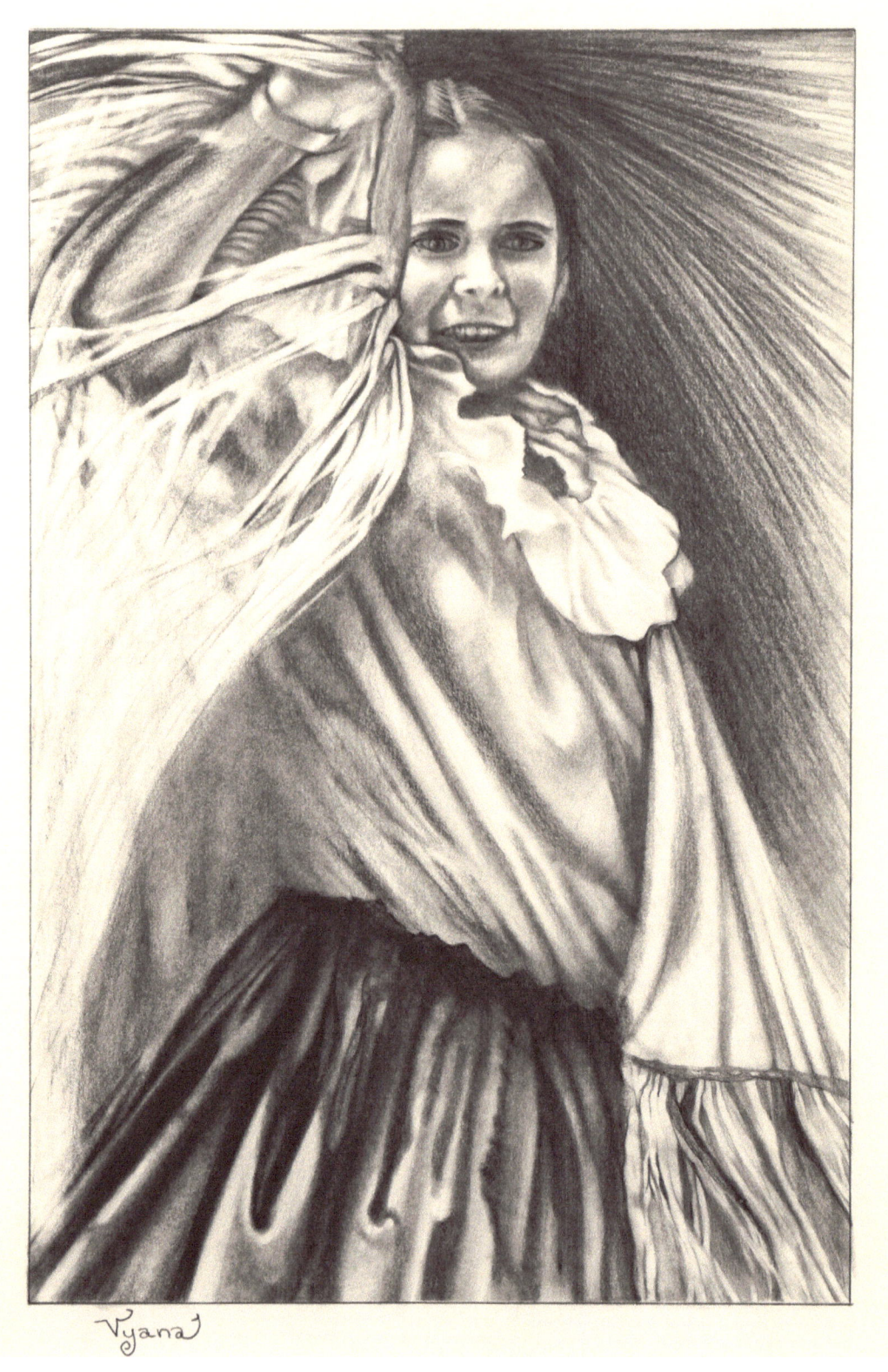

Vyana

Sensitive. Gentle. Tender

In seeking the pearl of essence
an authenticity "beyond love,"
a neutral zone is created that is in constant motion.

hiding & seeking

in staccato rhythms seeking royal blues,
violet-Red-ultras, i emerged transfigured.

in hiding-seeking dazzled by
sequined gowns spinning and twirling,
i emerged transmuted.

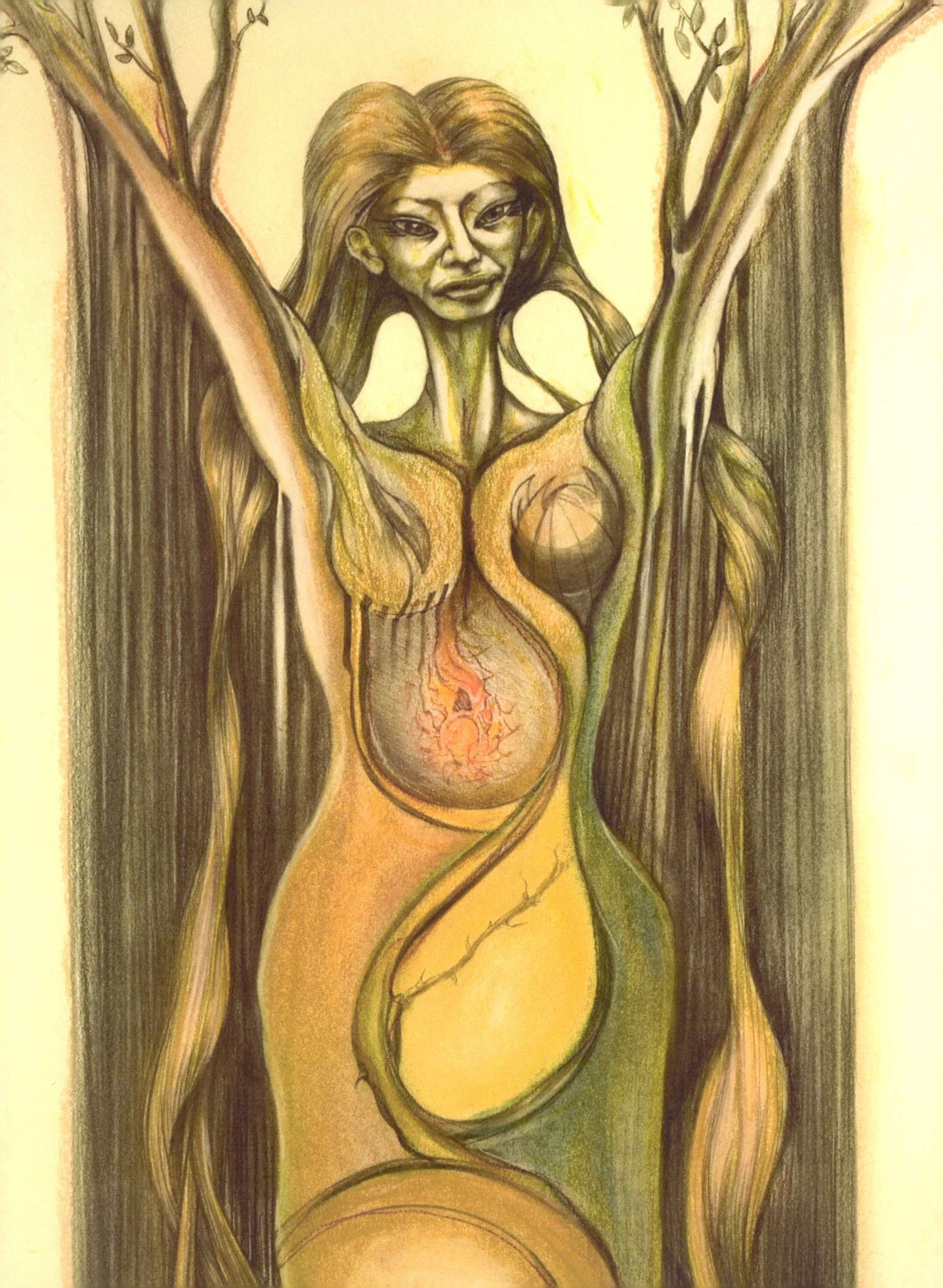

Spirit Tree

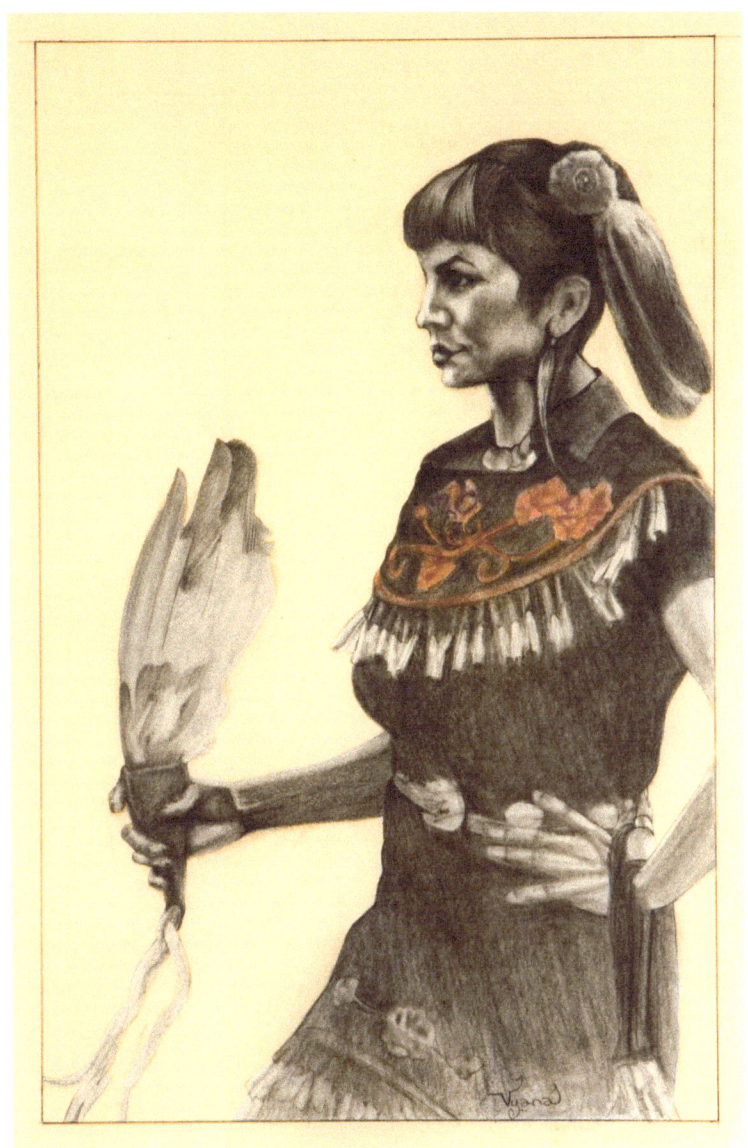

Empathy is not simply

"seeing into,"

but is seeing from

insideOut Other entities.

ahh-me-bahh aka amoeba

1.
this is a story of actually being one 2 many
of standing on the hemispheres of one 2 many
and even of no words none

so pondering the question, the question becoming the answer
and the question framing is also in the receiving:

a scaled down model of a grey Jaguar coupe engulfed in my memory
a monopoly board of the neighbor-hoods.
of frog men movies in grey and grey
of eating blueberry pies from off of grandma's kitchen window ledge
a lightening, and a lessening, it is siesta time
and when you are late you are late no matter how late you are
for now it is siesta time, is it not?

2.
as life is entertainment i do not need everything
only what i need
yet, why would i ever pay for entertainment?
huuurrrumph!!!

i am not stingy, but i buy everything i need
and my art is my entrainment happy for me

so when i dream i write in big magic markers
and in the morning papers scattered all over the floor

i read much, and much less than you would think

and with a different childhood i would be a psychological reporter
as a way of sharing patterns i see so differently

so if it seems crazy it is only that i write of that which is emitted
as recovery is not where it is at all
as it is all about discovery all and all

trust is easy as i make up my own rules
so i do not doubt
as i first accept
and then find out

3.
i noticed the best persons at anything doing anything
taking a 1/2 beat off of their actions
for it seems they know how to trigger-implode
through creative portals openings into locations seen not seen

and cha cha chaos is the secret of spirit dancing
so you can move to a warm climate and walking naked all about

so it is i now perceiving: tempo, timing, rhythms phrasing musicality
choreographing atmosphere creating expressions interpretations
with golden skin lotions painted
smoothing over bodies now shimmering

staccato sinuous sensuous serpentine-movements
of sheer translucence spinning posturings so expressive
with full painted red violet lips
gathering all with my pseudopods engulfing
nourishing me, my art, my life, my love, my loves
i write and write, and write some more
as all is well on this fine day.

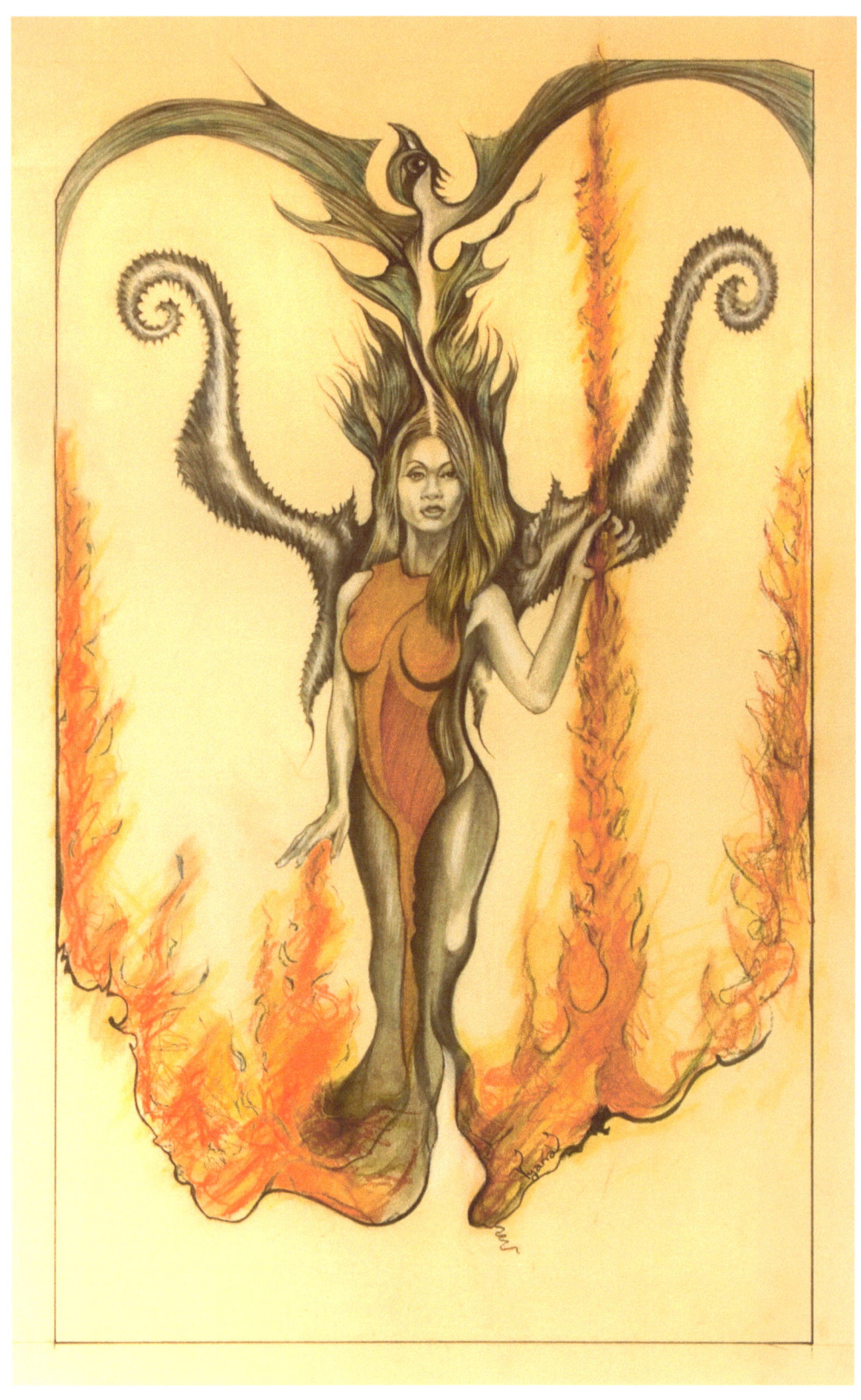

fire RITUAL fire

heart's Secret DANCING

looking in touching my heart's secrets
glimpses of images enchanted
speaking whisperings of passages of tantric secrets

meditating upon genetic codes in matrix crop circles
touching into hollow marrow bones with tendons changing

somatic techniques of
iron shirts integrating subversions into mega shadows
sparking into secrets of emotions dancing
of dancing shadows and emotions dancing

angry women archetypes of feminist paradigms shifting
subversions Workshop integrating
the hollow bones carrying somatic secrets

passages of integrations by dancing Shaolin shamans
caring of heart's secret-E-motions
the dancing whisperings of looking in

heartThinking, love is

1.
happiest ever, yet disturbances why?
my mind is exploding
hither and thither going waiting
anxiously abandoning me.
what a mess!

closing compressing raising
anxiety levels
feeling horrible
me despising me.
i am going crazy here depriving me of
so much possibility! Yikes!

closing my eyes i begin sensing the frequencies
of what confronts me
seeking the real in pure and true love
in a drop, a perception of oceanic vast color fields
with honey bees,
insects, and
arousing scents

endurance, cadence, and time lapses as fear of
abandoning self leads to
fear of abandoning friends

oh my, overwhelmed with ups and downs
becoming feverish with Phoenix fire rising from
the slipping away of layers of old skins
dehydrated burning

2.
a vision clear and firm of 22 years ago.
was it a searching,
or
was it a waiting?

a memory now beckoning me into
a possibility of you and me
from an Autumn scent of many Autumns past

impregnated into this Autumn scent now
not of expectations, strange, for it is a waiting
from lemon mist, sage sweet, and rosemary healing
as they inform me and invigorate into the presence of me
yet, a certain scent detected in transitioning leaves
lying dying on the ground
a sweetness of scent as if it must be someone's name
soothing
soothing
in crisp Autumn air
yet, beckoning Spring already to be,
yet far away

a step, a stop, a rock, a What?
in the Autumn-scenting leaves pungent and sublime
a heartFlower survives the cool crispness of the
ions free filling atmosphere, as if a heartStar in the night.

i find, i linger, it is we/us, not lost in the wonder of it all
just you and me,
my heart, your heart,
our heart2heart,
no you no me
only one

love is
waiting not ever more

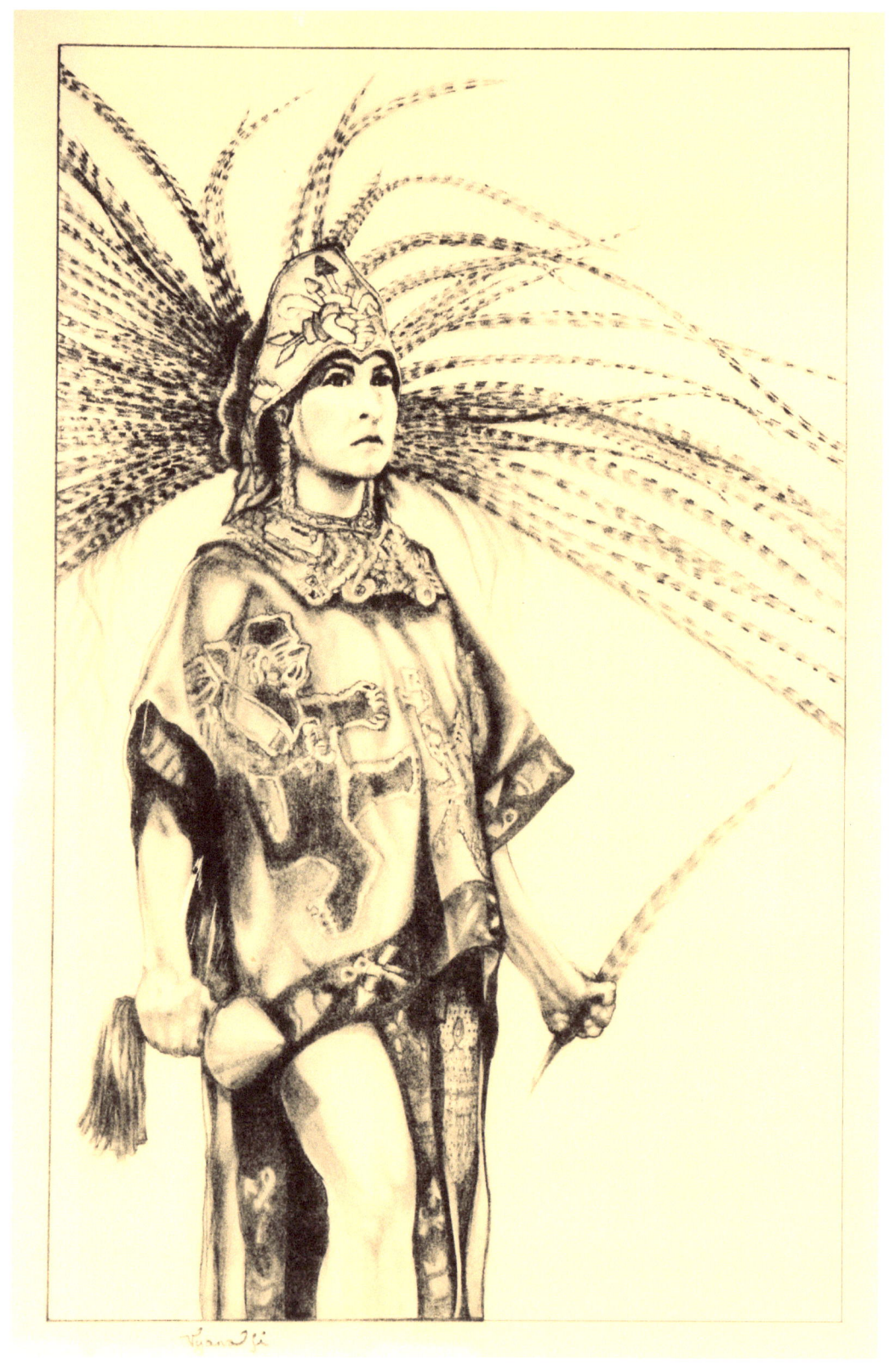

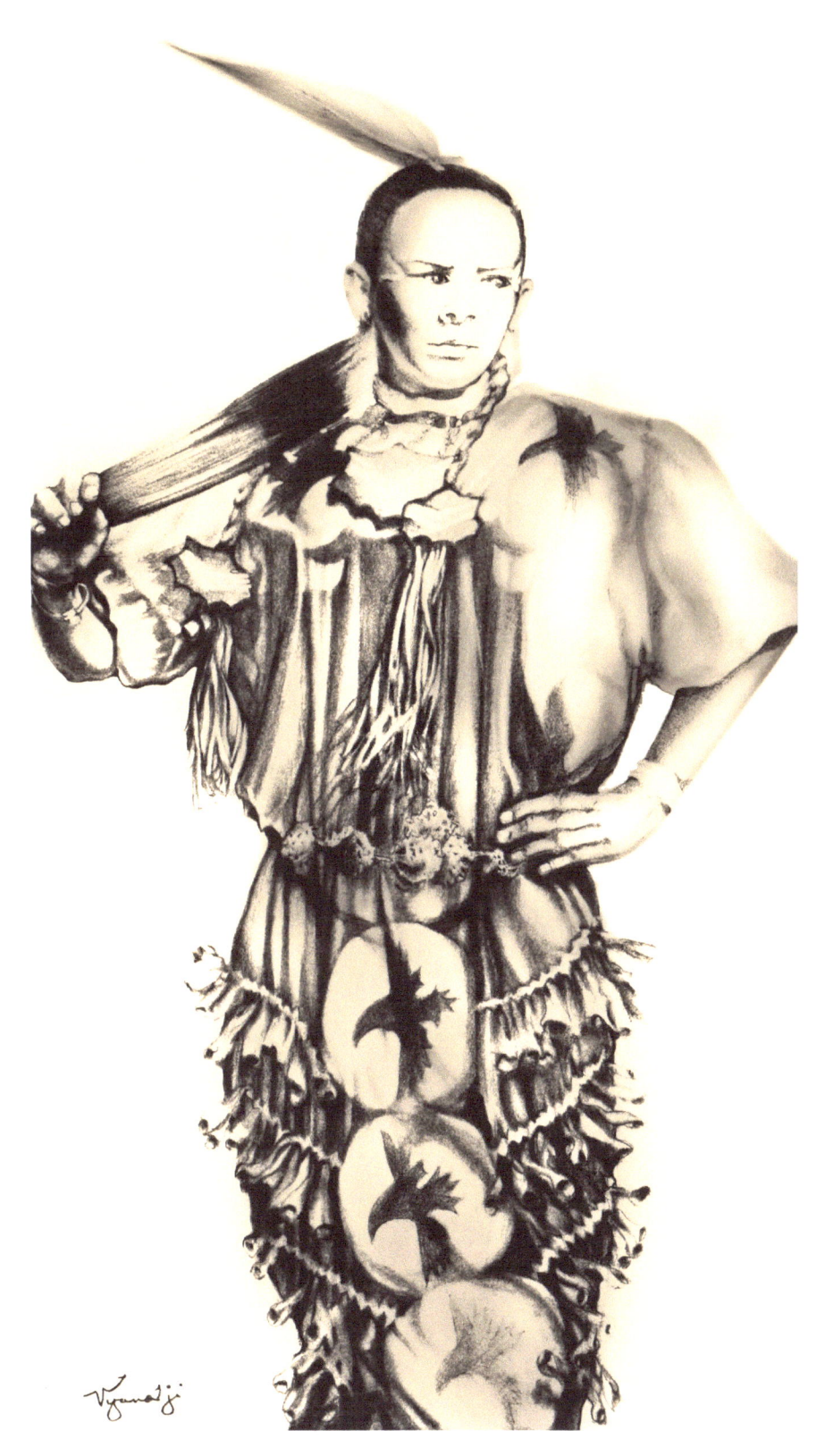

PART TWO

The Fool's Journey

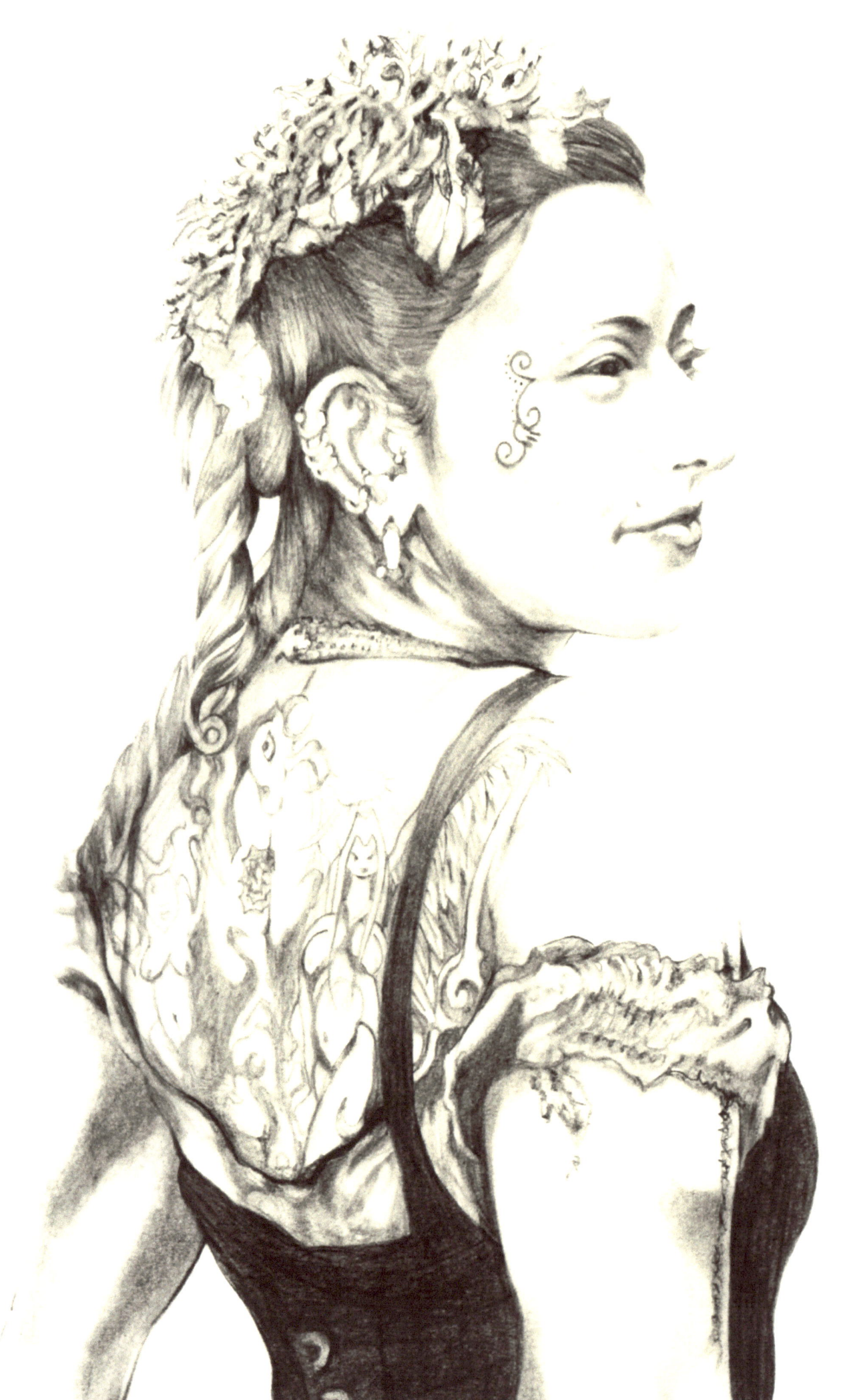

horizon's edge

1.
reframing everything
rain rain
do not go away

re-turn
quiet
alone
manifesting the Mystery again.

2.
finding self
what would i do
re-framing self
really, it has only been just a few hours.

patience, patience
draw, express inner rhythm outward
much to happen as weak express

be calm quiet
eyes return
sleeping with eyes wide open
day arrives
continue The Work
home again.

Harmonzing Opposites

The emergence of the sacred feminine,
and the death throes of the
patriarchal dominations and annihilations

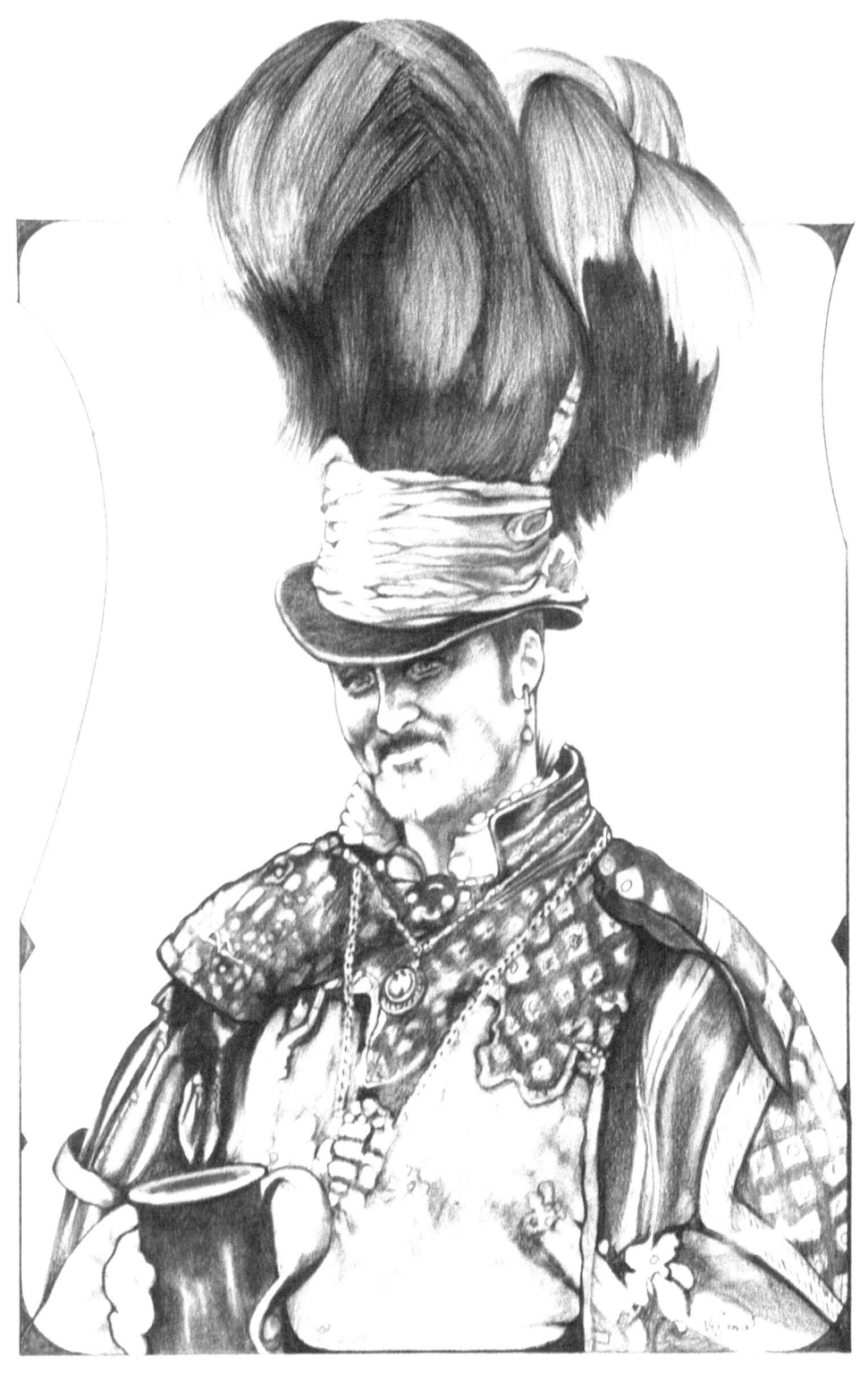

Racing and Pacing, No Map At All

1.
there were star charts i drew on the ceiling,
while i was a child then.

and then,
the fizzures appeared into the flatness of my ceiling,
and my wood-pillar bed post, well, was it a bed post, or a tree?

i grew and i grew, and as i ventured out into world the fizzures
appeared again and again as if driven by some unknown force.
so, i aimlessly wandered the streets
and noticed iron grate-grids along the sides of the streets.
and i noticed that i was different than the grates in the streets.

i was told i came from over the top, the snow-cap from above,
yet, i pondered, what if the cracks, like rivulets, in the planes
of the ceiling were on a similar journey.

2.
the world of longitudes and latitudes numbingly condensed
into my rock brain after all.
circumnavigating the globe, were these lines not there at all,
compressing my being into a hard tiny spherical shell?
i blinked, said abracadabraSomething and sank into the sea
with no maps accompanying me
into a world without maps?
so, pondering inside of me, what was the nature of me?
the map could not be me?
the tree was a bed post, or the bed post was a tree?

3.
there was a rumor that Humpty Dumpty had a severe fall
and fell to the ground marked by lines of grid-maps oh so firm.
yet, something may have happened, for i fell into the world,
with no map at, and,
observed that i had been deceived, for there were no maps at all
as i sank to the bottom of the sea.
and grew gills, fins, and what appeared to be wings.
so, with transfigured anatomy i raced and i paced with no luck at all,
for i had no maps at all.

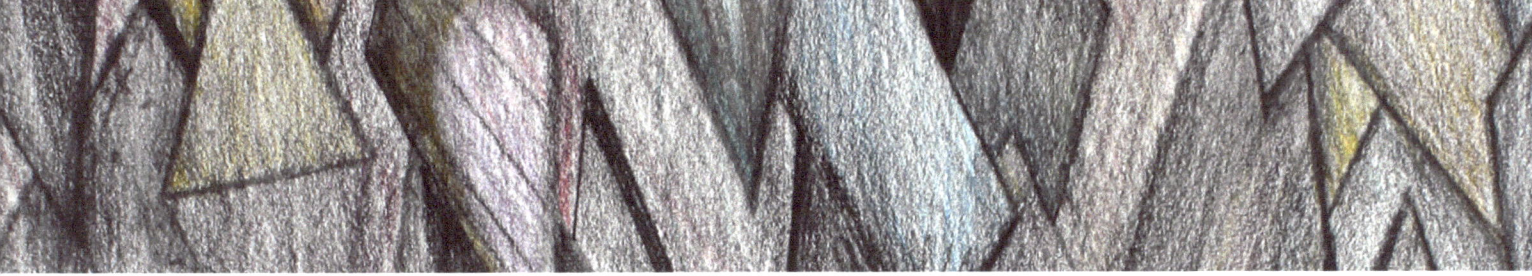

so, having no lungs, i journeyed and found:
no lines on a map, only planes and planes
folding, unfolding, and interweaving into
threads weaving and spinning of my consciousness unknown,
but 'felt' as an essential intuiting of my nature,
which will never ever be a map of the essence of me.
yet, of me, of iridescent light, phosphorescent fishes co-mingling in the
currents and waves of me.

4.

as artist wild creating the world creating clues outside of expectations,
bed post and tree trunk, what is the identity of me?
traces of something 'other.'
i slept at nightNotNow seeking a secret nature:
my nature within Nature.
traces of something of intimacy of in-here and out-there,
epistemological origins of my consciousness
my travels, joys, and travails
vulnerable trusting unique
no map, i was a wilderness of person-me
of sand mandalas simply expanding and deepening
in glowing dark-lights with improbable beings.
echoes and resonances in my wombSpace
racing and pacing under the sea.

5.

revivified, now walking the streets immersed:
iron rusty sun radial patternings
ragged edges
rectangular iron grate-waves within, like the surface of the sea
blue arrow spray paint on the iron heart of the street
squirming centipede legs creeping crawling
striation parallels edged in concrete planes
speckles of green-grey lichen dancings herethere
yellowed leaf stains expressions of what was,
and what was not
dappled rain dropped surfaces of sheer delights
twin rivers of ripped and shredded textures
running to the skies
shredded canyons and organic moments in-between

rivers running with counter cracks sideways
cracks collapsing closer and closer farther and farther
grid lines juxtaposed as prisons defined
dissolving cracking openings
neutralizing hues diminishing
schools of grey-brown scraggly fishes
green moss velvet skin carpets
flaking skin flakings
limestone chips overlaid with pine needles sharp
soft slick wettened skins of river honed rocks
interstitial patterns opening consciousness emergings
inducing me into spasms of delights.

6.
cracks and twigs twisting and challenging me
to decipher their codes of hidden meanings
limbs severed from me-Tree stepping over sand mandalas big
with intertwined iridescent blood stains blue and green on the ground.
speckled stars of limestone chips of softly lit greys
speaking to me
of insides and outsides exposed as my skin slides away
opening meridians tender and raw all over me.

Can this be me?
unknown in the unknown apparently that of which is that.

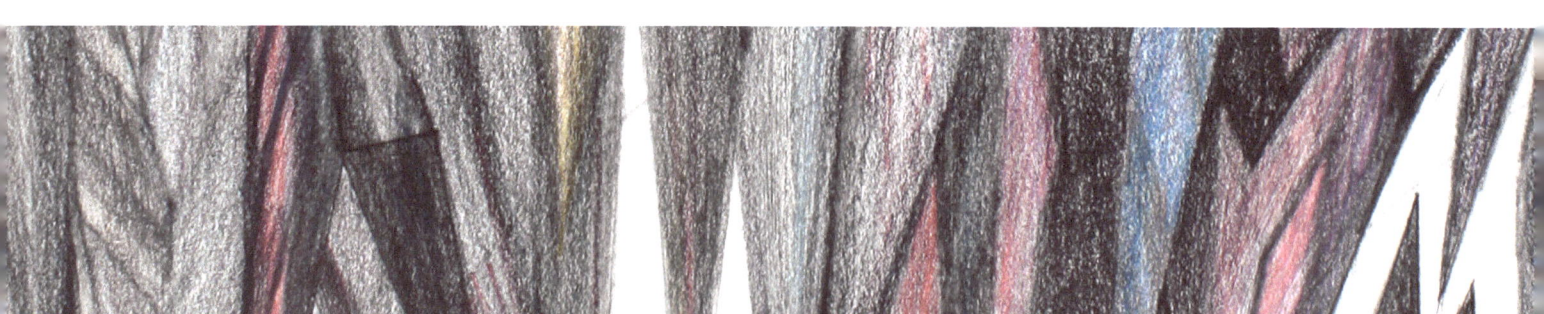

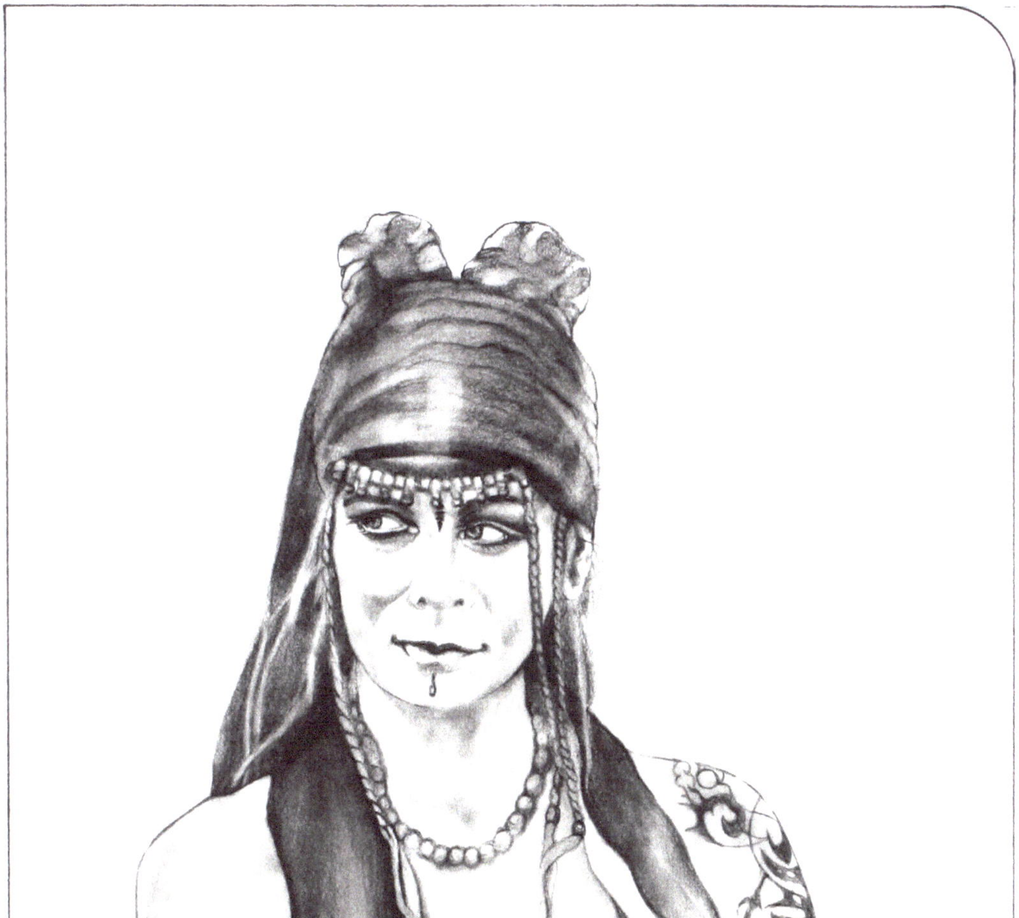

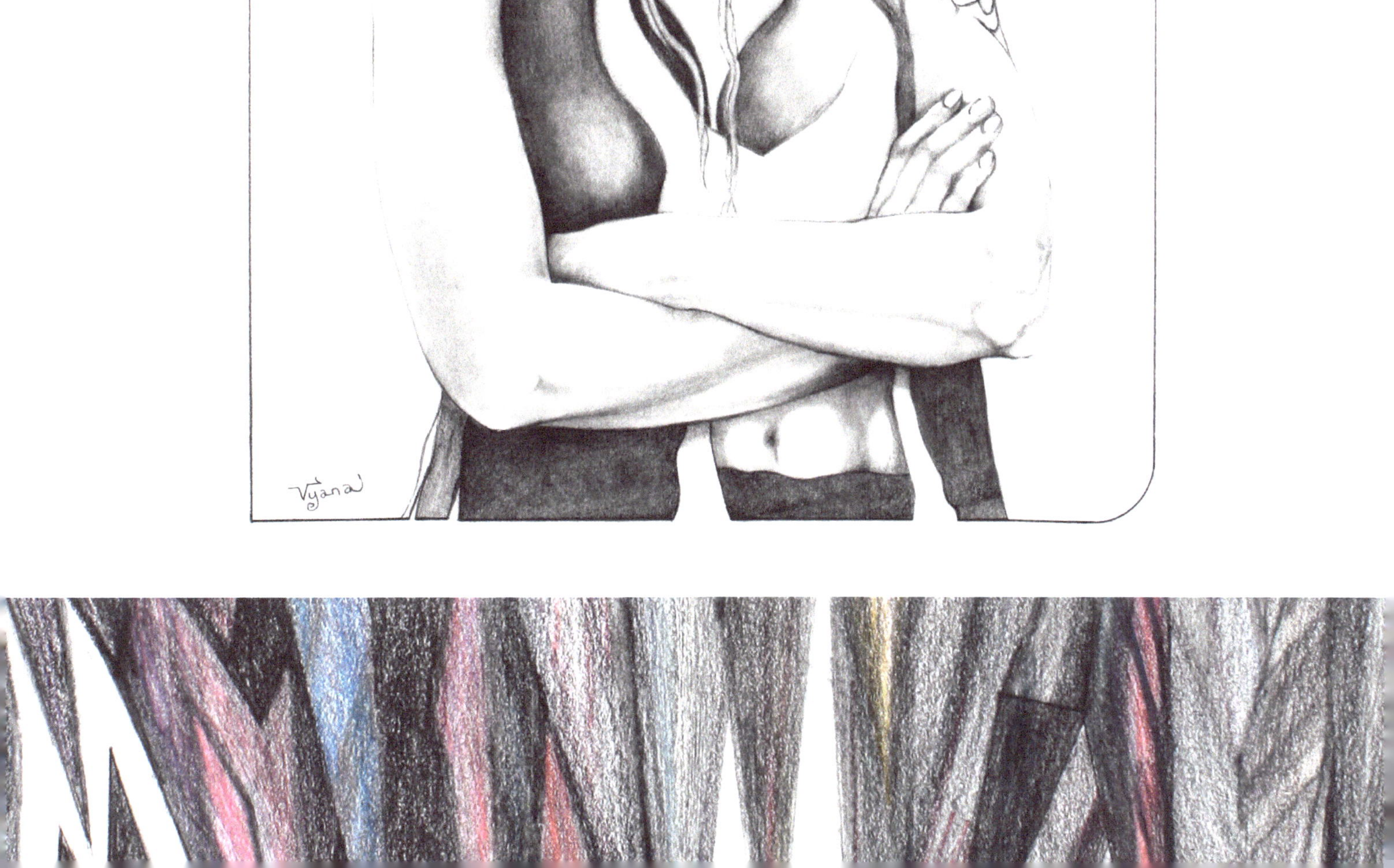

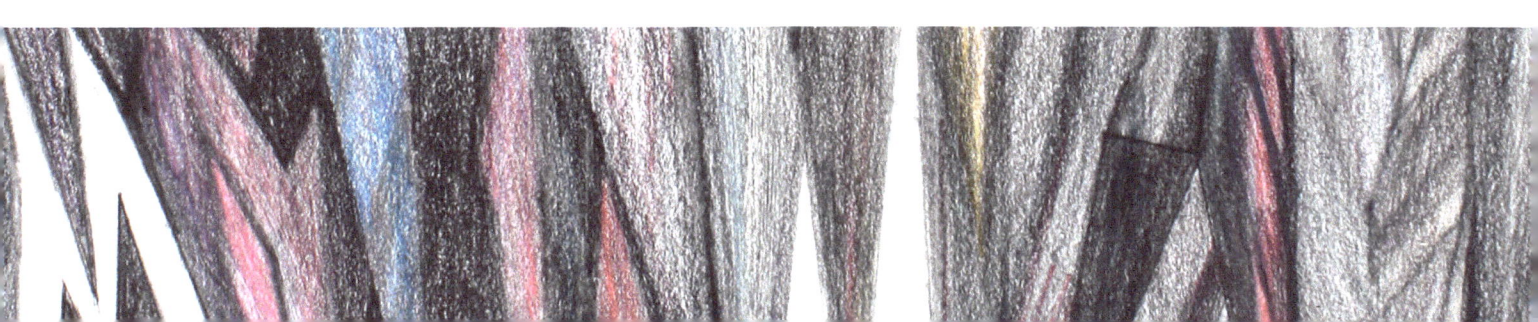

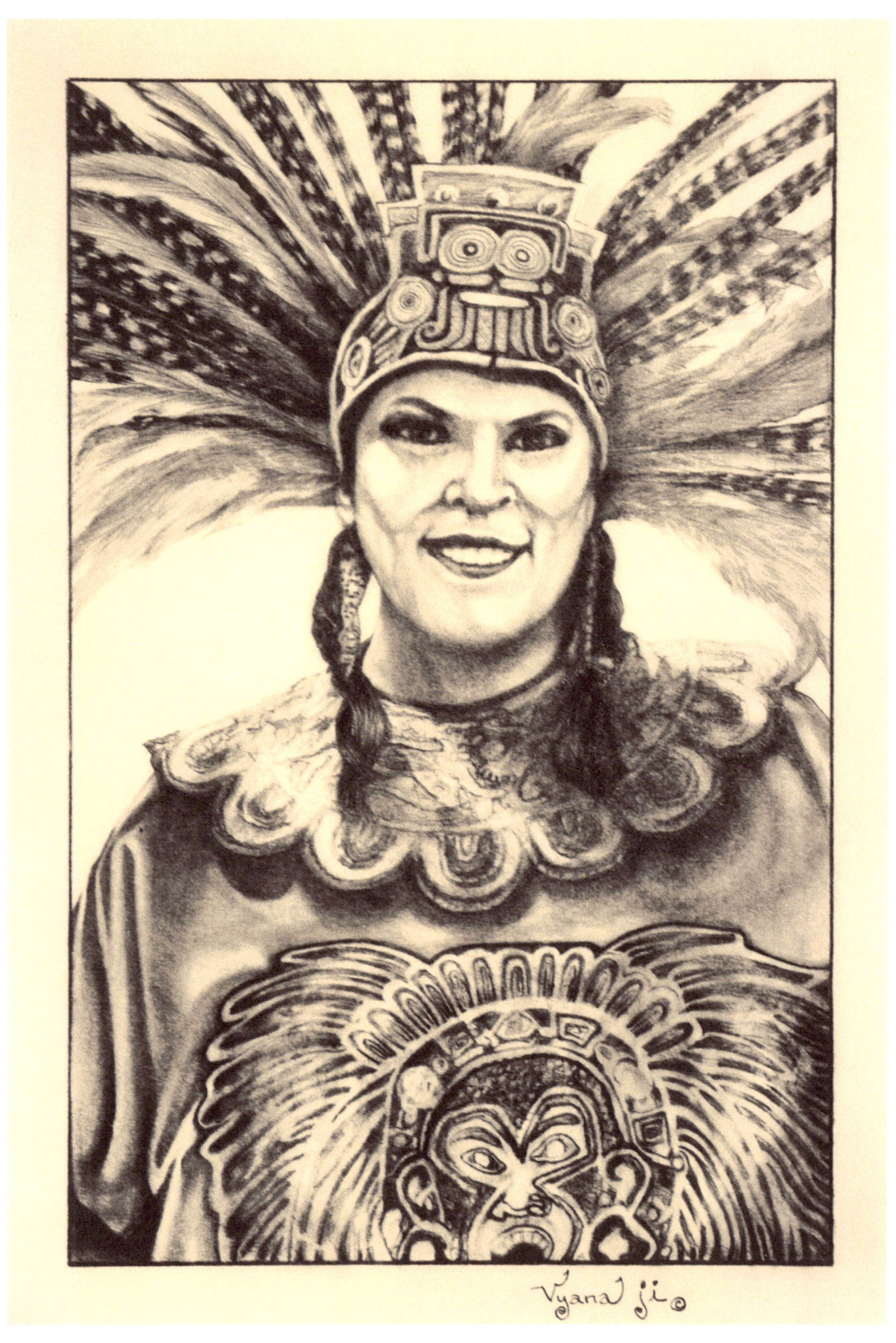

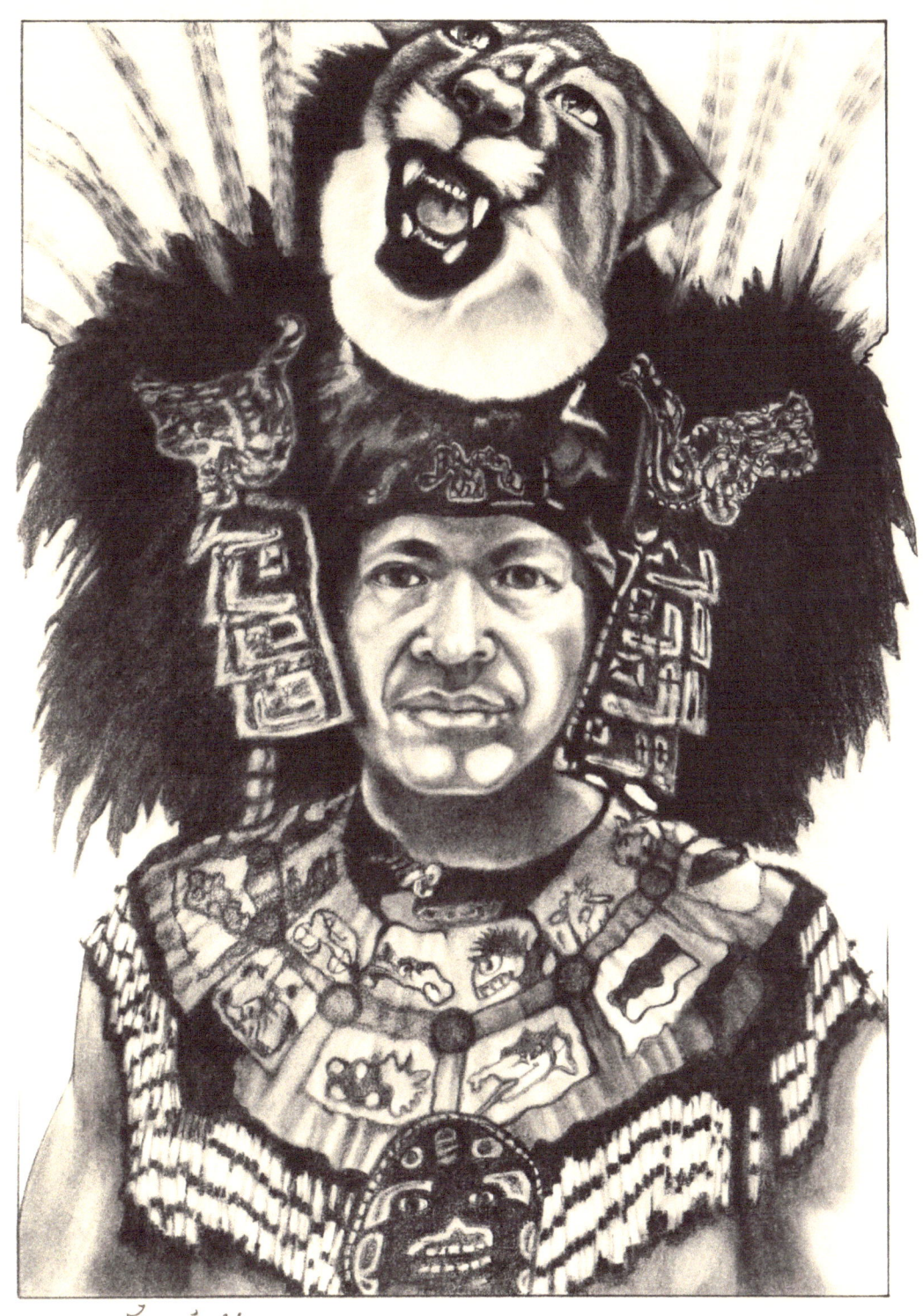

lost treasures, dear Mother India?

1.

dear mother india,

i was one of you
many times
way back then

strange, even in my silly astrology chart
it is said that this is so,
but i knew
when i was born here far away
as a yogi, guide, and teacher again
that in my ancient home land
that you, mother india,
had been decimated and raped
dearest good mother,
and my sorrow was buried so deeply in my soul
i waited and waited to return again
and i have done so in the autumn of my life
one more time again.

2.

your treasures have been stolen
and now they are given away to the
highest suitor and bidder.

the price to you has been horrifically immense.
you are a shallow and emaciated figure
of what you once were in your glory
and effervescent. a shining glory
unlike any other to the world
unique and diverse
sacred and sublimely connected
to all that is, for
love is
dear mother india.

3.

i walked in the bowels and the heart
of you upon my return to india, stayed with humble
and beautiful people, who said:
"come to my house," and i did everywhere
i traveled with my big back pack on my back.
i found a 3000 foot deep canyon and traversed its
crevices downward to be greeted by a leader,
a shaman with two wives, and they fed me well.
although i ran out of drinking water
the water leaching out of its rock cliffs was
as pure as can be.

i slept on an outdoor platform and was
immersed in the glories of the heavens
with no sounds nearby, and even
no airplanes in the sky.
i danced and drummed with your people
and your children,
and i am a drummer and a dancer of a
different kind of indian where i live
far away now.

i climbed the switchbacks sooner than later
and found once again the narrow road
which widened wide with
throngs of people and animals alive
as i walked and walked.

a screech, a thump, two sounds
for a truck broke and shot off the narrow
road and flattened a woman in her sari beautiful
carrying precious water to her home.
another mother, of course, but a mother just the same

something died in me too at the fright of it all.

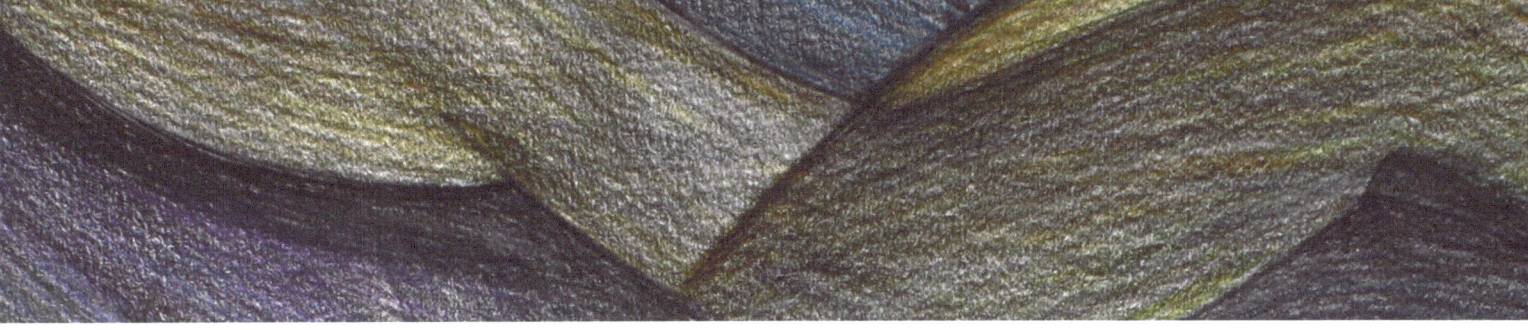

4.

i found my way returning through pune finding it
so harrowing before me with auto factories and endless
more of nothingness meaningless and became bored
again,
and something unnameable died in me again.

then i resumed to walk through a large tree shadowed
street
and i slowed and slowed almost to a crawl in its daylight
semi-darkness.
the street was blackened and thick with
oil and debris crushed into a slickness of
oil and occupied by 3 festering black crows
searching for something i do not know,
but the 3 warned me again:
treasures lost, treasures stolen sweet india.
i covered my eyes

5.

i was not..............there lost
i just could not find my way
but it was not of
the treasures that were,
but only the scraps that the 3 black crows
had informed me about
on that thick mat oil trash slick on the ground.

something immense died in me and india in those days,
but the people beautiful sustain me then and now
for their generosity of spirit fed my body and soul.
i picture those kind people even now
in my moving picture mind.

those kind people nurture me, feed my spiritsoul,
but never to return for you, mother india
you were given away,
yet, you are here with me now and
paradoxically my neighbors the door across the hall,
they are from india too, in the physical,
yet, unlike me, i can only live in the spirit of what was
now

6.

to mumbai to fly
i stand upon a flowered covered reservoir
and enjoy the summer heat,
and a muslim family very large wave and smile to me
i remember them all very well,

i look above and see ravens circling in the sky and
told that they eat the flesh of those who had died.
i shivered in the heat of the day
wondering if that was me the flesh of the day,
and in a way i was no longer really there, but
now already living in my endless wonder-filled dreams,
yet still not departed.

i finally was happy to be home with you again
dearest mother india
i am even now so grateful for the scent of you
for the glory of you hidden hidden hidden
to those who no longer see and hear your
lilting voice, and you do nurture my soul
dearest mother india i want you 2 know,
for i, too, have become a flower from the
excrement on your streets and your lands.

i was treated well
by your people
i love them so
i love you so mother india

love is my gratitude and my offering this dark night,
but i see in the dark
and feel the soft rain 2
and the gentle breezes
that have commenced this very moment
to cleanse, to heal, to inspire me
oh, mother india
love is
love is after all
love is

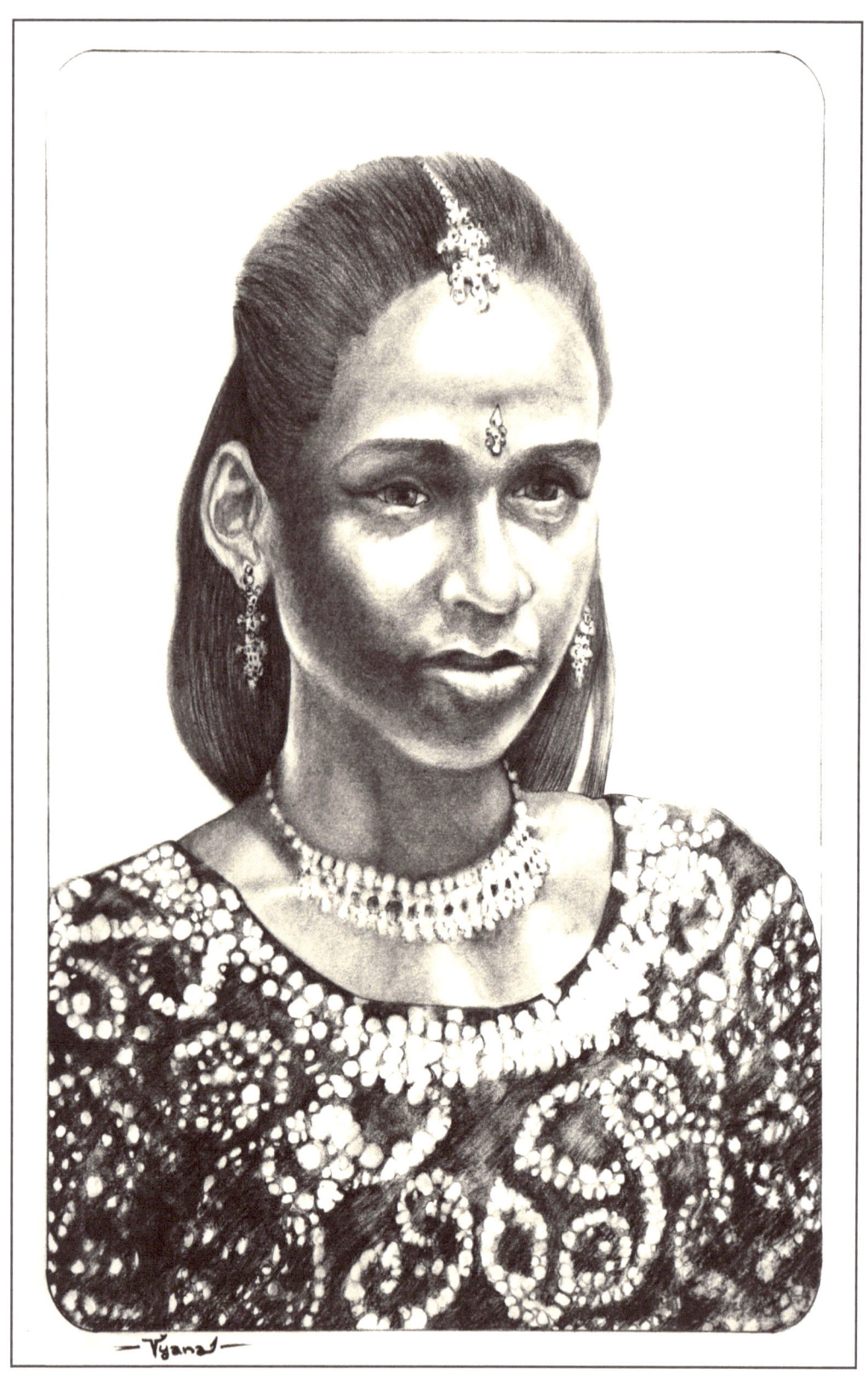

A young woman without words

Our energy leaves our body
and expands until it touches another

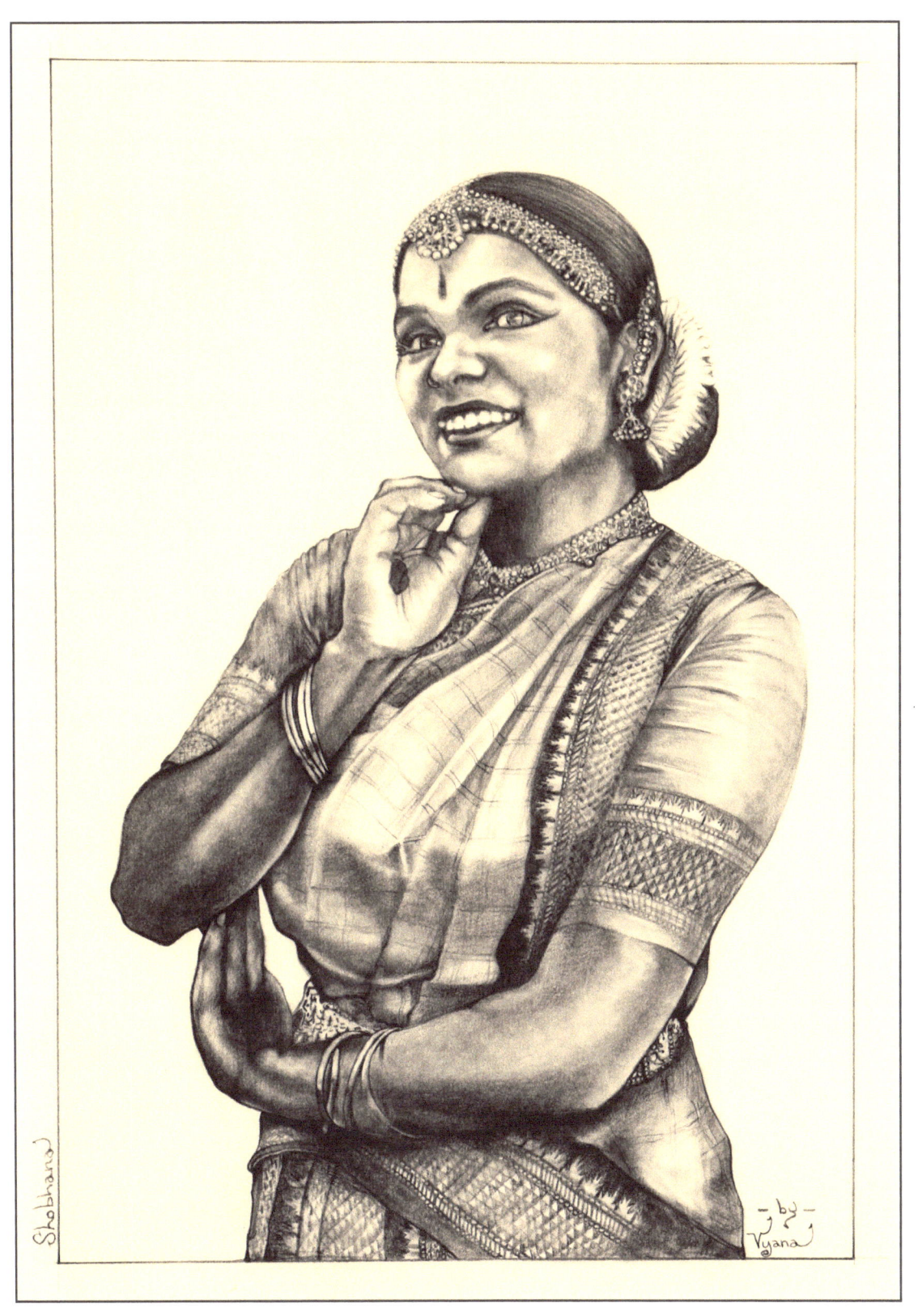

Then, we are blessed in return:
Circles Sacred.

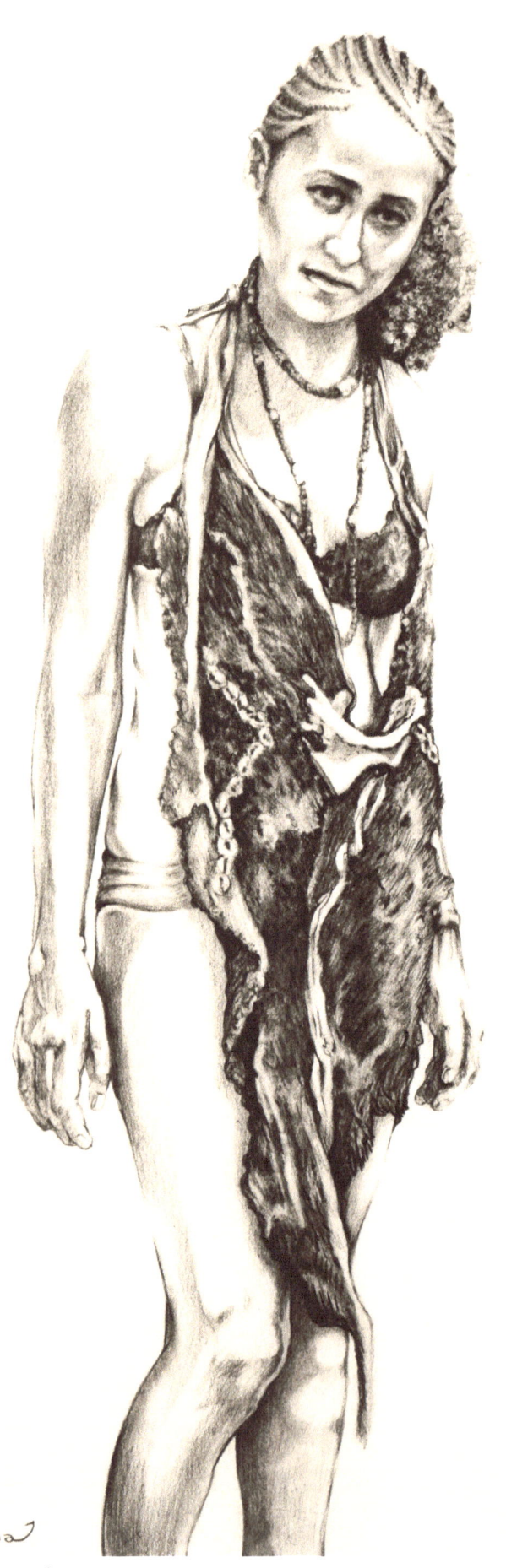

Shaman Beautiful

duo resonating feminine

Voices transcending

more powerful

than healing

innocent

ancient

youth

mature

crone

spirits

two

resonating Voices

one

two

one

not two

not one

not

two

inflections

zero inflections

pure

all

two women

continue

thinkingHearts

precious hearts

as two dwellings on the river

rivers of light

rios de luz

alegria

joy

jubilation

now

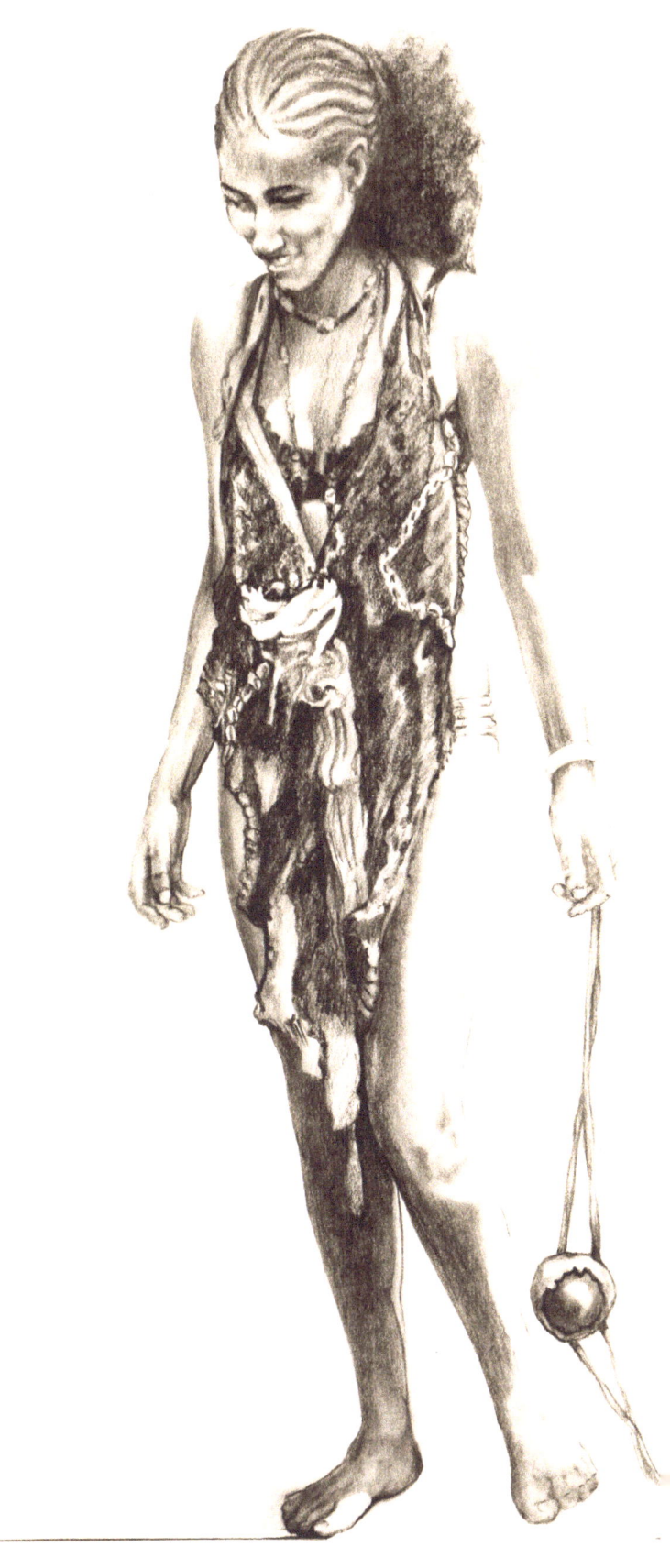

seething paralysis

1.

A true story? Yep!

I thought that i knew crazy? No way! You will see after following this craziness which would make for notFunny fiction.

Cautionary note: you are listening and have been forewarned that this is a storyNotPosssiblePossible.

Really? Not possible!!!

13 days of what?

13 days of crazierCrazy

This has to be a joke?

This is not what actually happened, right?

This Modern Age story cannot be real?

2.

we arrive at the airport to depart for London.

Ummm? Her credit card, her driver's license, and her passport all have different names!!!

missed our plane.

she takes one hour calling 1-800 numbers.

yep, if you are catching on here,

we depart to jolly old England on the next flight.

this is to be my first authentic experience as a space-time

traveler with an encounter with the imploding universe,

but, true story, remember, my imploding brain universe.

3.

NOW in the center of London.

so, to save money on the hotel she instructs me to wait

in the street, actually down the street a little so, be aware,

she can save a few pounds aka dollars.

you see, i am the problem while all this time i thought it was her, Gaynor.

so, this story will just spiral from here in no logical order:

she informed me quite assertively that she had been her

high school's homecoming Queen.

she definitely made sure that i was aware of that point.

Yet, botox treatments revealed her to have more of the face

of a long gone prize fighter.

we journeyed to many locations: twice to Scotland, twice to Germany,

once to Holland, and then the return flight from London to the U.S.

on our first trip to Scotland, i did all of the talking because the business owner, originally from Argentina,

was a sexist according to her, so i had to prepare him for her brand of toughness.

on every occasion possible she put-down with endless diatribes every woman in our radar fields. Not so, ironic, really, that the women were actually more attractive than her. I became very familiar with the term, poison darts, on these occasions most frequented.

so, the question now is, "Crazier than what?"

as i become dizzy spinning sinking into a vortex of lost hope.

we ate at a fine rooftop restaurant in London on a most pleasant

sunsetting evening.

so what?

she steals 2 bottles of wine hidden into her purse and coat,

after accusing the waiter of taking them away before we were done.

and there was a missing throw-comforter as well. what?

4.

by now, this was not entirely unfamiliar behavior as she managed to force her way [me 2, eh!!!}

into private clubs and restaurants.

Oh, did i mention my part in all of this?

Yes, a recently new mental health problem identified simply as:

seething paralysis.

at one fine Indian restaurant she casually informed me that she had the equivalent skills of someone with six ph.d's.

5.

i am never late, late, late.

10 flights, 10 1-800 phone calls consuming minutes than hours.

we missed all 10 flights.

remember, the 'seething paralyzed' one?

yes, patience looks impressive after having

passed Acting 101 long ago, does it not?

spent time in Harrod's after closing hours as she convinced them to stay

open because she was going to make a big purchase.

really she measured and photographed purses so she could rip-off

some famous brand names.

enough. enough. enough.

yes, sorry, there is more more,

but i know i have had enough,

even if you have not.

lessons [maybe] learned?

i can travel anywhere no matter how challenging

'seething paralysis' is my version of 'losing it.'

patience is probably only 'seething paralysis.'

when offered an all expense paid European excursion,

i should probably ask, "At what price?"

life reveals itself: "Let me count the ways!!!"

Willpower supports you as all actions are opportunities for awakening consciousness.

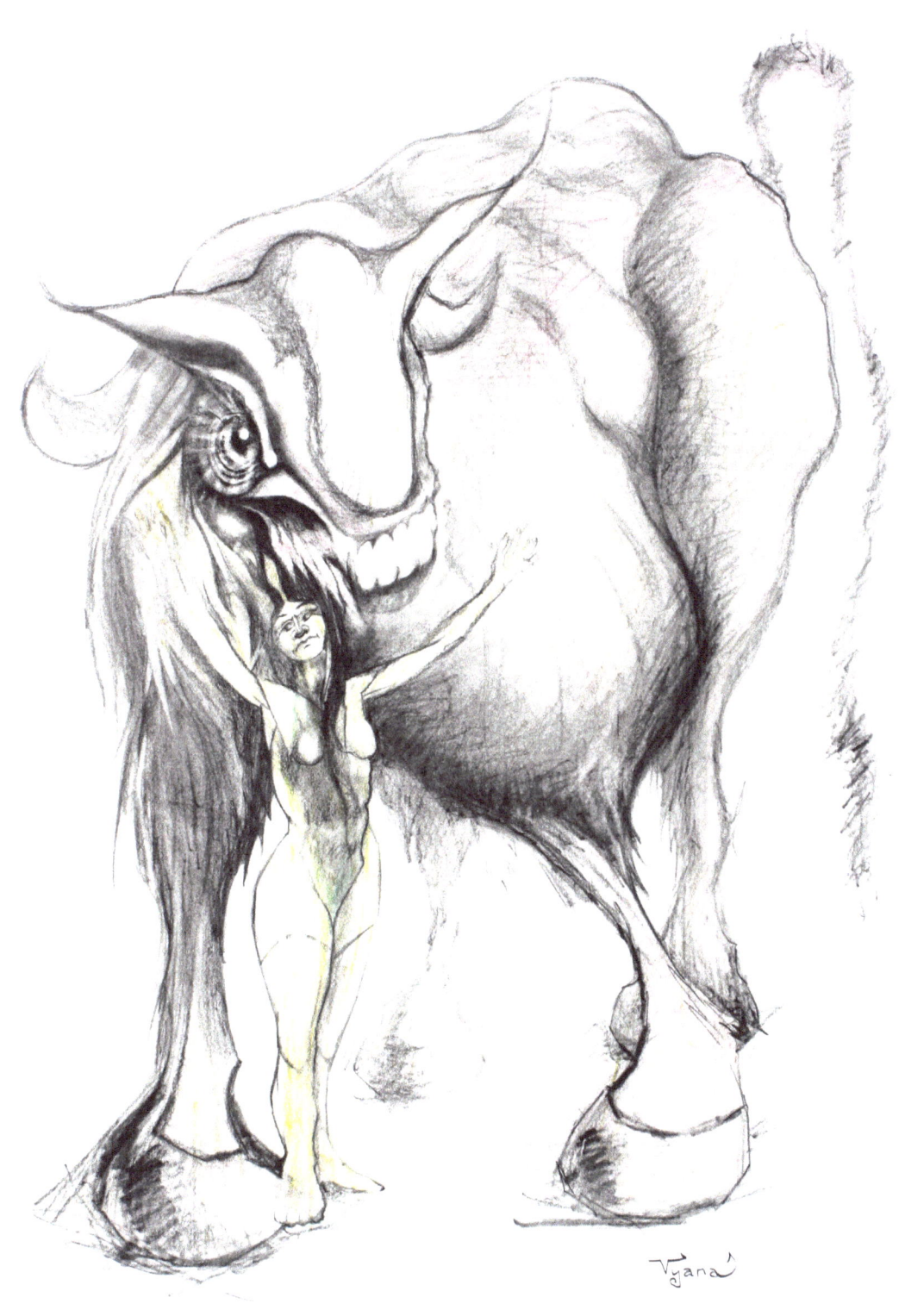

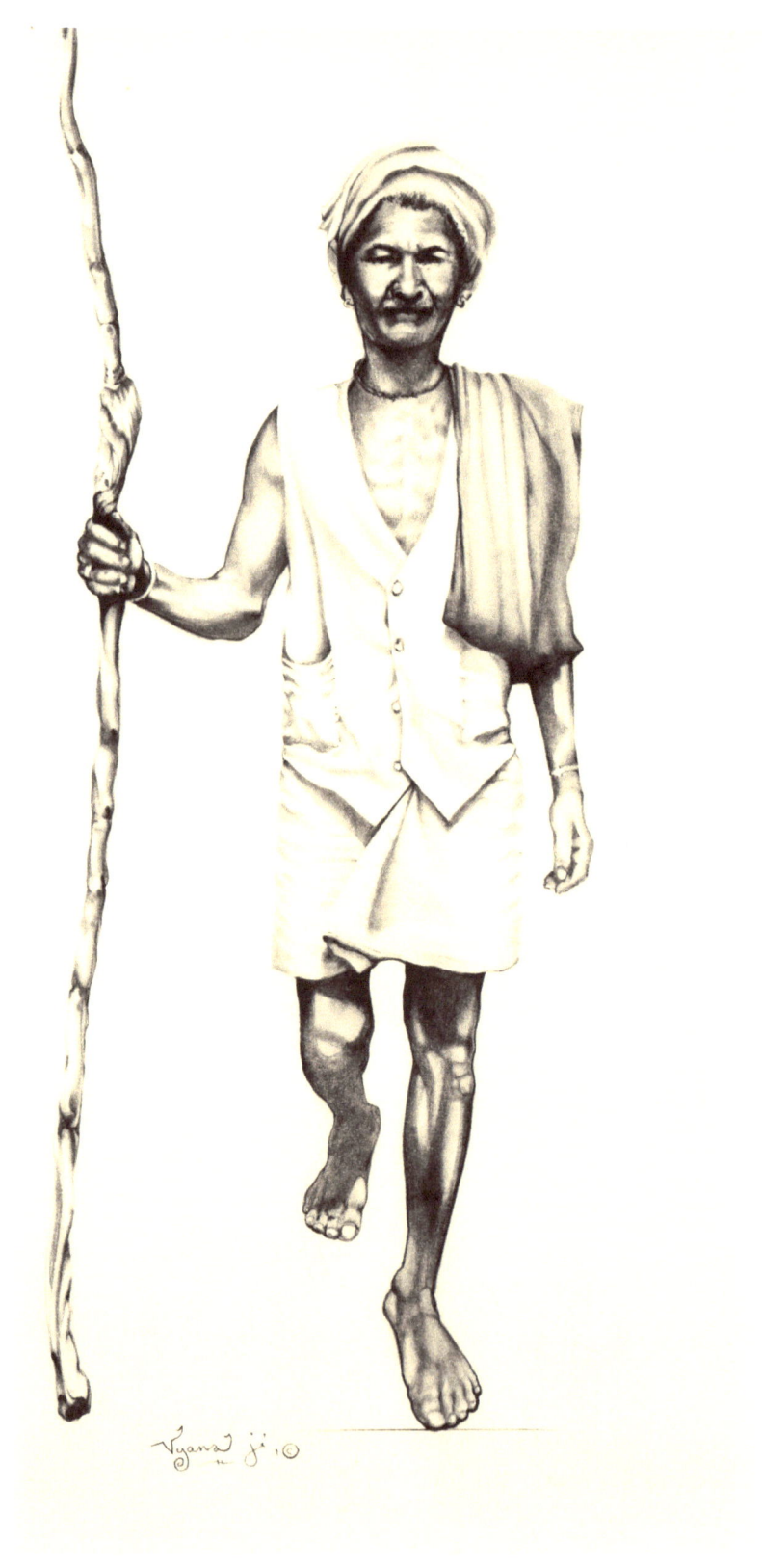

56

hiding hidden me

a facet of my personality that intrigues me
about the personality of my personality
as i play ignorant uninformed me
or, is that an un-formed me?

ha ha ho hum the Thunder Beings on the
Western horizon chuckle as they chide me for such
frivolous superficial redundancy.

i love the speakings of Parker Palmer,
for he in-formed me years ago about:
"Bringing people into speech."
well, of course, that seldom works,
and, ordinarily backfires!!!
ha ha ho hum

so life goes on, ha ha ho hum
like a dwindling river soon to be
a dry bed stream.
yet, i wonder still, "What is on your mind?"

oh, i forgot, you were scared to ask?
oh, i forgot, you thought asking was inappropriate?
oh, i forgot, even that you forgot?

so, "What was it that you forgot?"
so, "What was it that you might have asked?"
oh, i see, i understand now!!!

desperation

feelings of being lost ... feelings of desperation
of the journey unspoken.
the journey lost to nowhere — i linger.
i become hollow.
i wait and i wait.
i now long remembered
there is not another way.
it appears

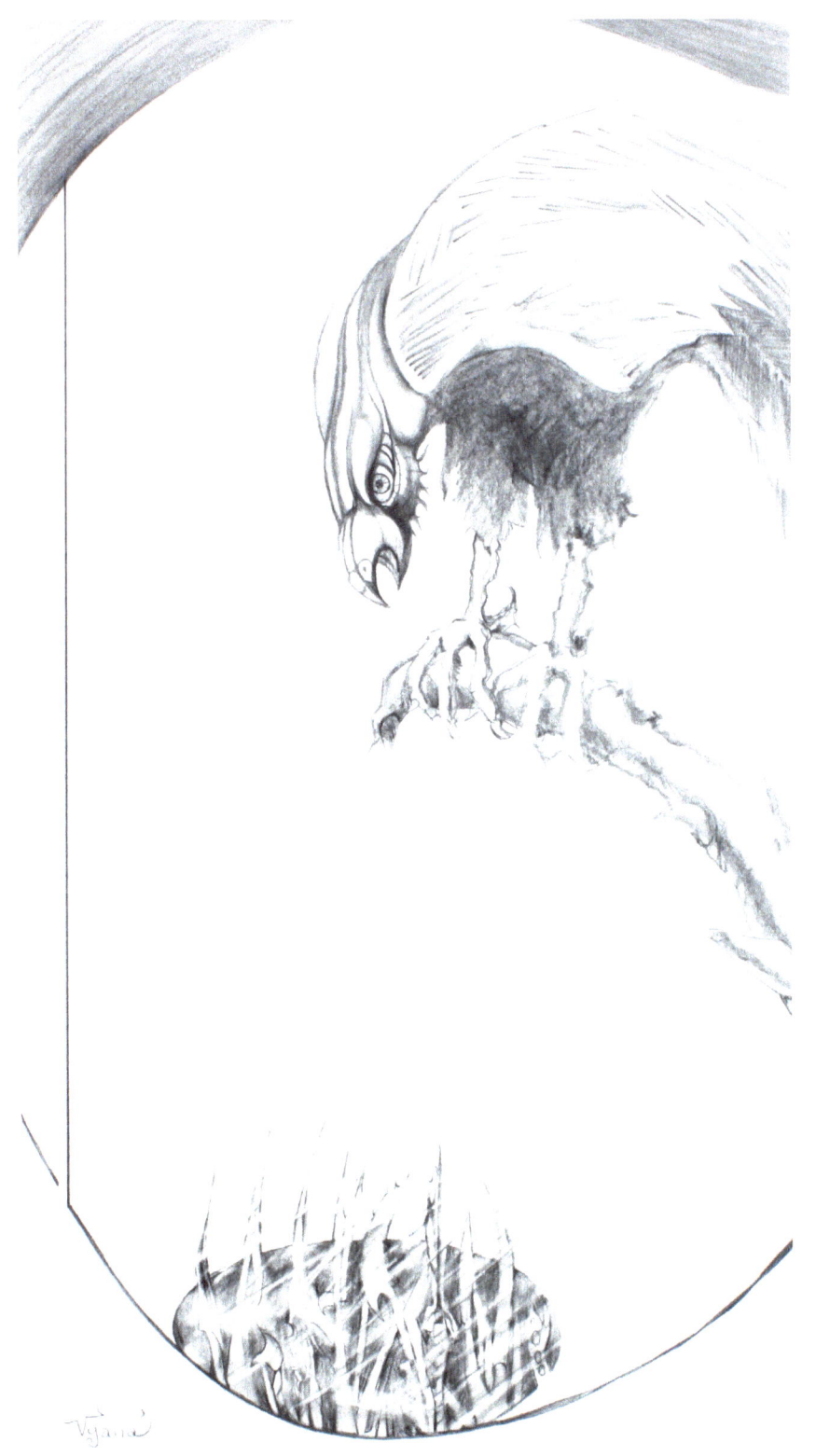

my life ended

was a freedom writer for Amnesty International
got a list each and every month
responsibly wrote letters acknowledging what?
those souls illegally imprisoned
almost always tortured as well
sickening how these two coexist
shocking and surprising how those letters sent
released those illegally imprisoned and tortured 2

you, over there, those of you who do such things:
exposure is your greatest fear
that is your real enemy.
and, guess, what?
the letters so often work
release is secured.
is that not amazing and spectacular?

yet, for me my life eventually ended, so very sad
i could not separate the abstract, yet, so very real veil
that seemed to insulate me from the terrors of the victims
i became more and more tortured
more and more tortured
and created my illegally imprisoned body and soul
i was losing vitality as it was seeping from my spirit, my soul
i was sleep-walking days and nights,
a somnambulist, and my soul was becoming twisted and knotted
ever more constricting my heart in yet another prison
yes, one of my own making
and my soul had now been marked
i was no more

i left, i resigned, for i was no more

a ticket, a flight, 24 hours
in Mumbai now at midnight
dust everywhere in the seething heat of the night
a few dull street lights
dust in the air, dust like a drizzle of soft rain back home
children playing soccer in the cool seething heat of the night
dust as grit grinding my teeth,
and i try reluctantly to cease my breath
i wonder, surely, i have landed upon the moon
fully occupied by spirited spirits playing games
can this be? I mean as in, can this be?

i wander and wander and wander more
listless days and listless nights
into the bowels of India and it's open sewers
and it's open hearts and i am befriended
conversations proceed
and more conversations proceed
their word petals of flowers on my heart
my heart proceeds
in the dustHeat of motherIndia
i am lost, and i am like the lost and found
in the library back home
but listening listening oh so quietly

many found me
and i questioned
and i listened
my heart opened
i became a flower
because of those friendly conversations
forgetting nothing
accepting all
sorrow and joy
whole and healed
i looked down and there
was my soul in the depths of my heart
never to cease ever again
love is ...
that is just the way that it is
love is ...

The Giant and the Marionette

As ideas become more and more dissociative
they separate people, induce fear, and are sometimes
used as idea-excesses to hurt,
or even kill, that which is "thought" to be
different from themselves.
This is xenophobia!

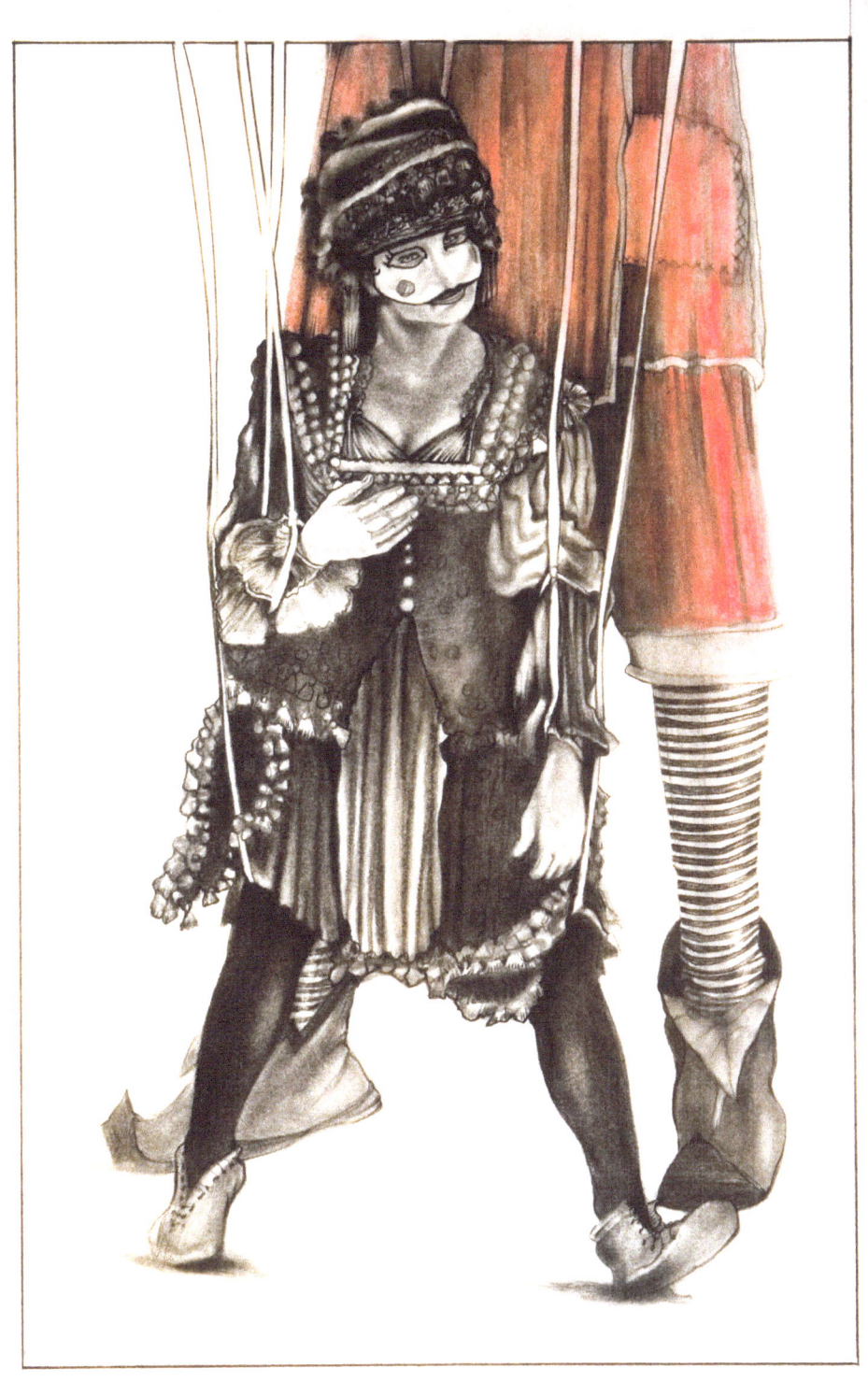

Vyann

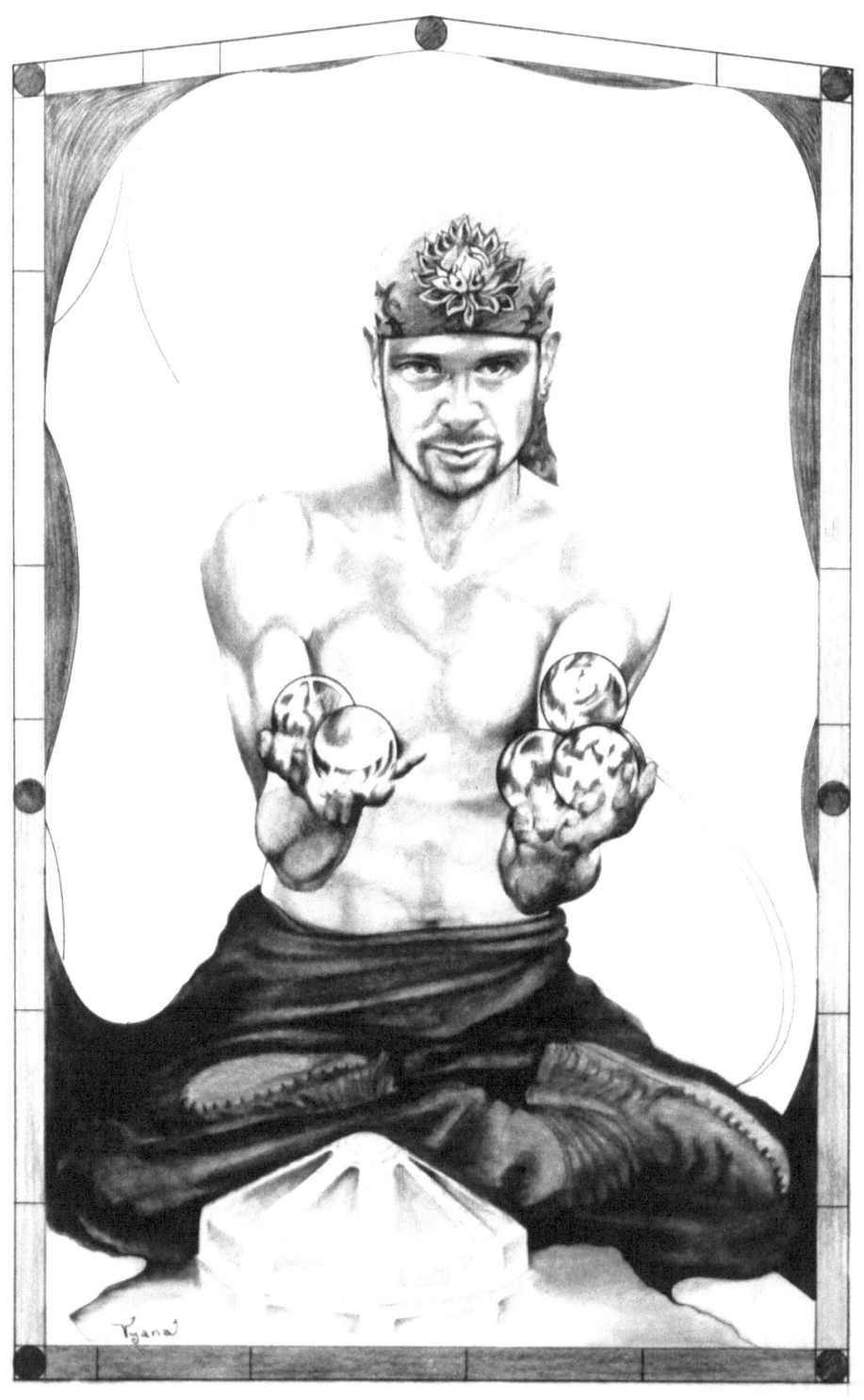

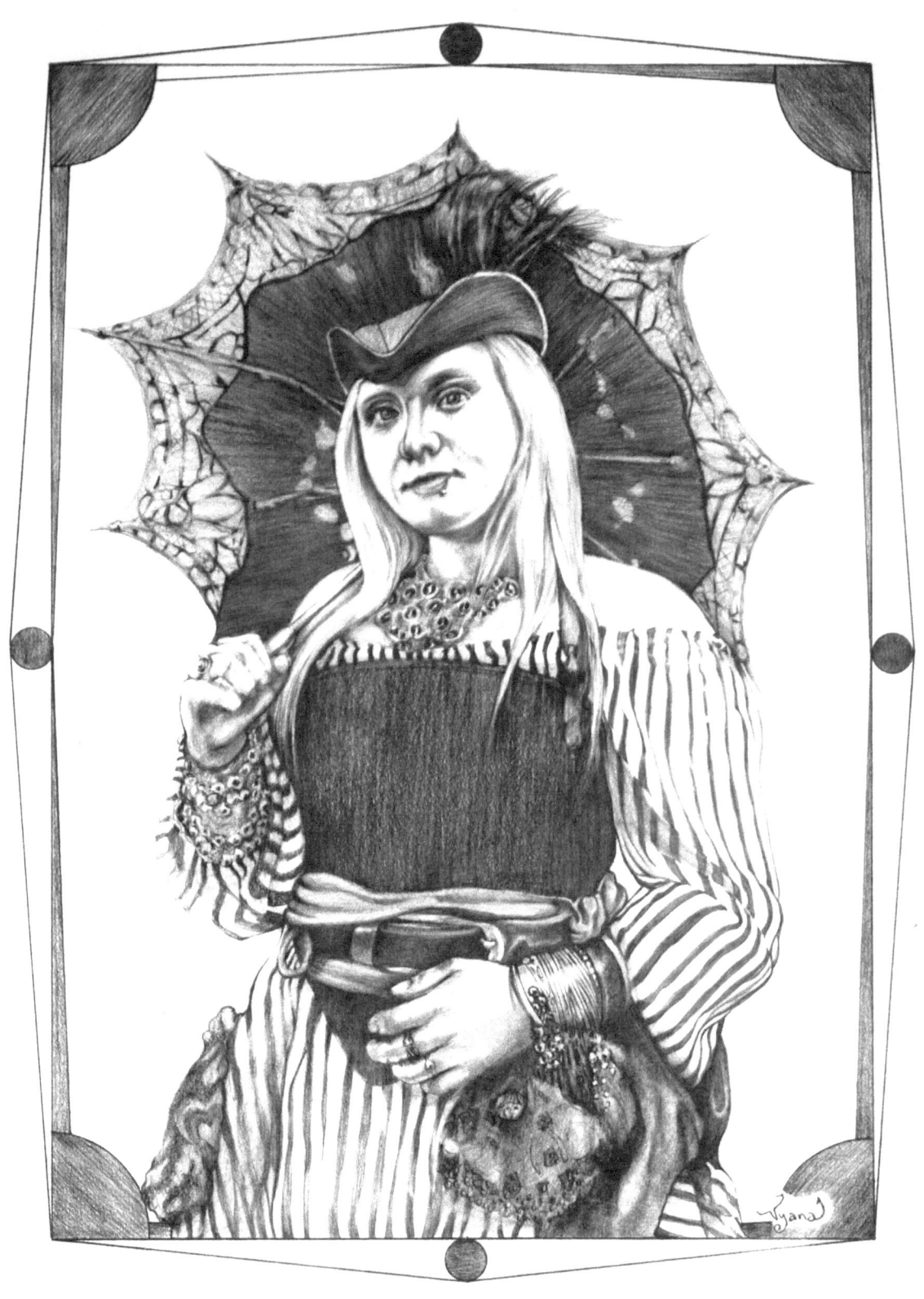

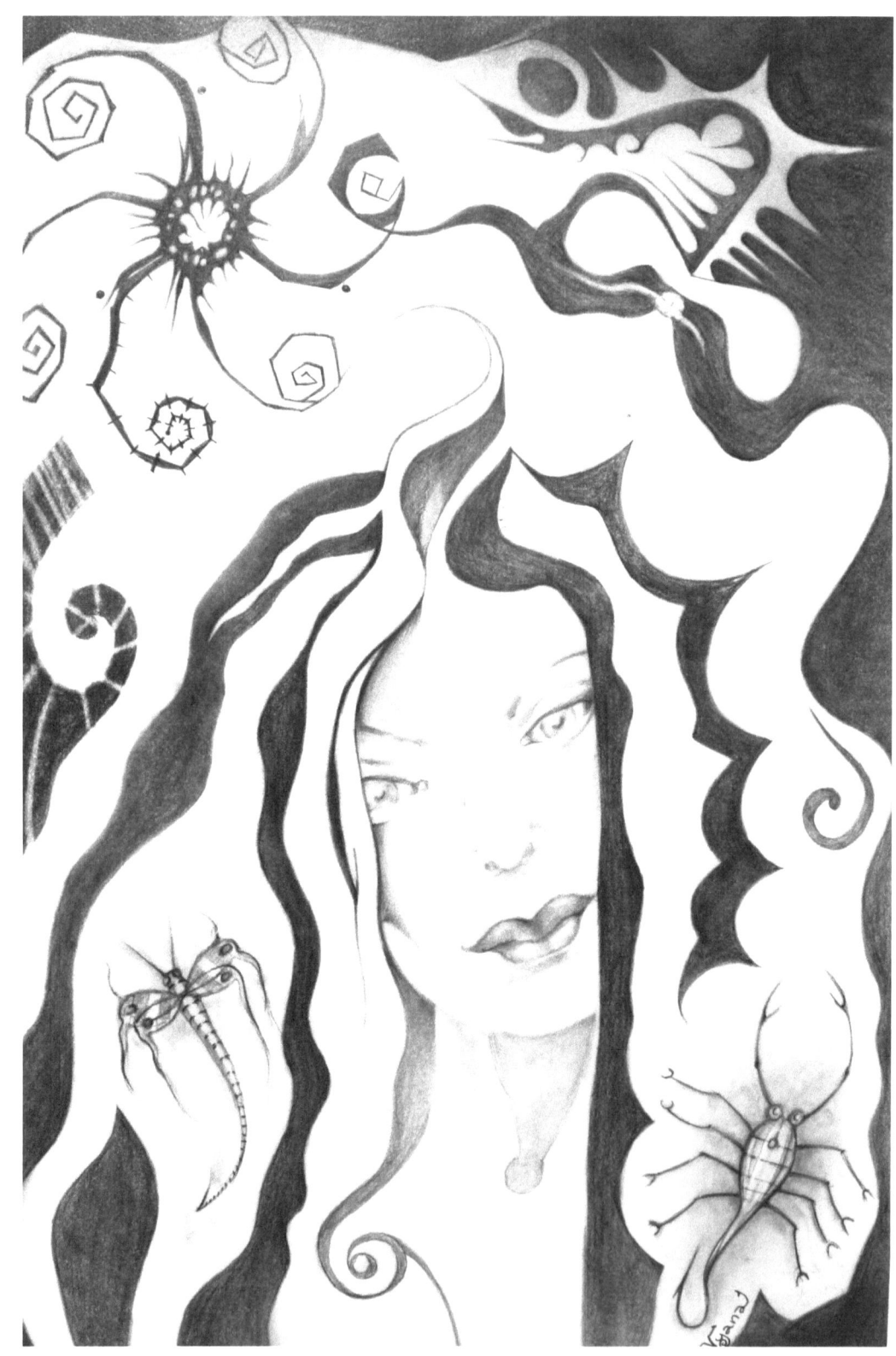

The Price of Human Suffering

A spoked wheel with a long broken axle
has become half buried in the sand
and grief is now time-bound, spirit stops,
and yet, the dancing must commence again.

# of what i did not see

1.
you speak of "tears of sadness" to me
yet, today i shall speak of joy to you anyways,
but, that will not appear that way at first
glance at all.

today i shall speak of a short stocky Mexican mother
and her 3 daughters
14, 9, and 8

and, this is a story of not so long ago.
it is their story, but, now, it is also my story,
and they know not of me slowly walking down
the side of the street
as i observe the four of them
a diagonal path
crossing the street

2.
a shocking stopping as the 14 year old of polio
collapses down to hard street ground a
half way crossing the street
in an instant she is picked up, re-assembled,
and escorted beyond
the middle of the hard street

me, stunned, tears of joy down my cheeks in
oceans of tears sobbing
engulfed in and drowned in a moment oblivious to me
destroyed
dismantled
wondering
if i can re-assemble this pitifully stunned me.

i shed ... tears ... of what i do not see, if only of sadness,
but i see only four hearts
joy of joy
heart2heart

love is ...

Presence

the incoming waves recede

fears recede

your presence emerges

into an oftentimes fragile world

you become

that which is greater than you were.

then there is pure love

as you see the truth of YOU:

your own love for you ....

this presence of you ...

a love so deep for you ....

beginning

again.

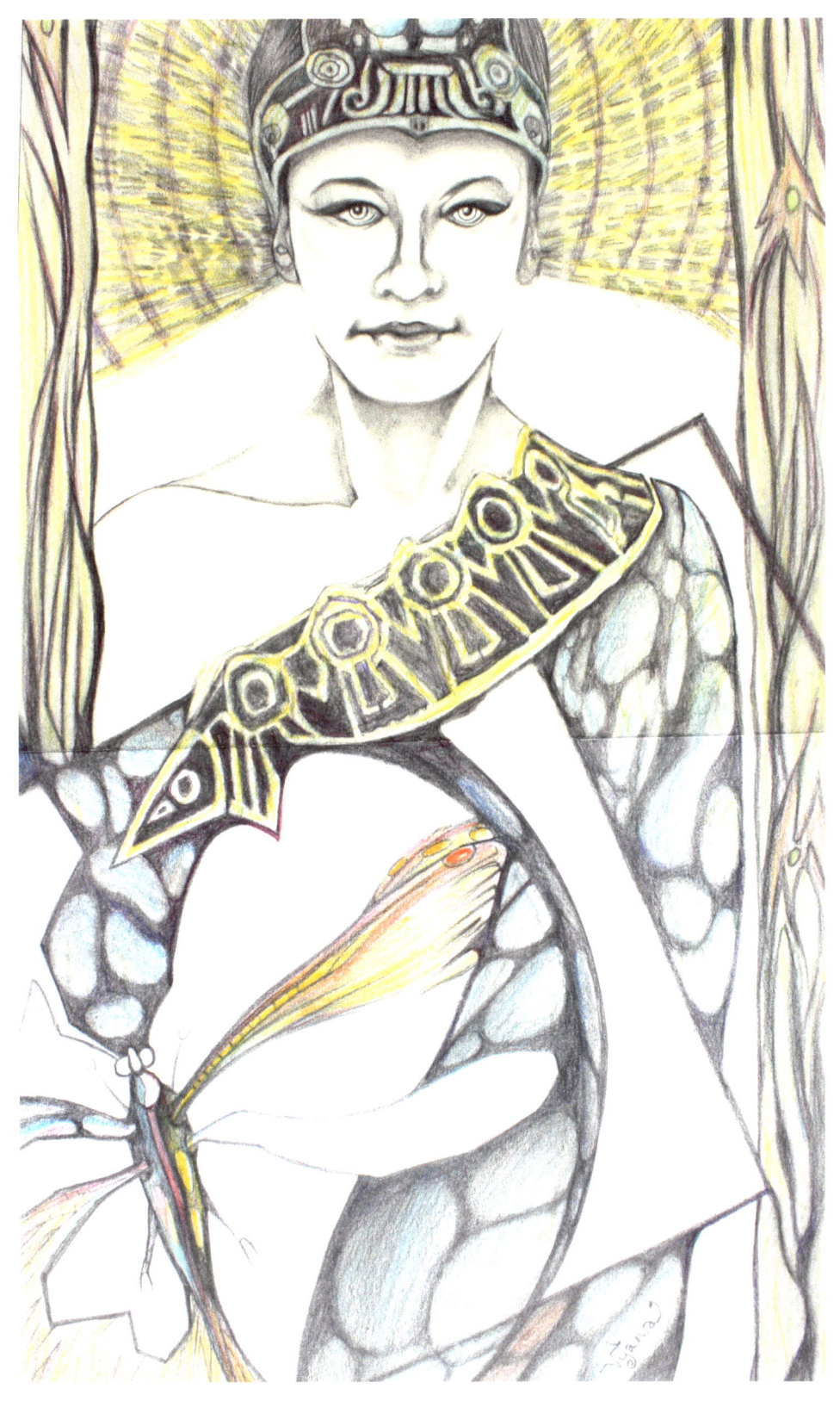

3 in the Morning and the Rest of my life?

1.
I was asked about what happens at 3 a,m.?
funny, even lame, question for me.
for i awaken, i write images from my meditations
i prepare, i expand
i breathe the imminent fireSun into me.
i breathe the Moon into me soon not to be.
3 in the a.m. is not the issue with me at all.
the issue that appears in front of me
is my un-lived dreams.

next there appears an intersection, a fork in the road
but unlike R.Frost, i walk both roads.

i teach, i guide, i travel, i wander, and i wonder
trapped in a body not of my own making.
humorless from birth i was trapped in many ways
learned many lessons
and still living my teaching as my dream still fulfilling.
so, how to live my un-lived dreams?

with no sense of humor i am as a void with no voice,
so i shall try at being a not so timid me.

2.
a walk in the dense city
an obscured sign down the street
a vision, nay, just a sign, but what a sign!!!
no, not a "sign" a sign on a wall.

I said: You gotta be kidding Clown School?
and, yet a smaller sign below that sign: enter here through
this very small door decorated with flourishes of colors.
so, i kinda skipped between the portals transcending
as a dancing Fool as in the Tarot.

3.
it has been awhile, it is almost semester end almost completed,
What?
I am on probation?
so very troubling i know
for i did not see it coming before my very eyes
humorless and shy after all
bribes not accepted,
i commence backwards to 101
then, 2, there was this issue, yes, about my clown car!!!
it seems many clowns entered my Granny Apple Yellow-Green car,
but not all returned, and just when i thought
i was doing so well in 101 lessons???
what do i do?

4.
the Clown Directors accused me of having forgotten
and repressed the voices of me, they called them clowns!!!
Big Trouble now!!!!!

so, you wanted to know about my book on book tour?
yes, a book that got me into even more trouble!
No kidding? Yes, No kidding!
here we go:

a. be un-reasonable, not reasonable.
b. your life will be consumed, transformed, and you will rise from ashes.
c. to ask is lame, to be open, be re-spond-ability so you can receive.
d. get to wherever you are going 2 hours early to write and read.
e. acupuncture Meridians are rivers of light. so do not be a sofaVeggie.
f. do not compromise or repress your feelings. 'too" is not real.
g. if you have a little car you may have bleeding gas lines.
h. to disturb passivity is to disturb the knowledge-you. Rage More!
i. choose to disturb the universe because it disturbs you.
j. coexist with you, those A-Round you, and the Universe.
h. seek the fulcrum point for beauty, empathy, and harmony. All days!!!

Belated News:
i have yet to pass Introduction to Clowning A-Round 101,
but that would not surprise any of you, eh?

.

the 'Other'

i have these passionate connections with those who see themselves positioned in life in a category i refer to as the 'other.' Those 'other ones' appeal to my 'other.' I, through me writing rhythmic juxtapositions of words and phrases, desire, shaman-like, to link our power to the modern world.

I write to create fluid, juxtaposed relationships that disregard the conformist labels. So, as uncomfortable as it makes me feel, there is an intended provocation, desired engagement, and a disturbing of universal harmonic flowRhythm-sound-waves near and far reverberating, returning, disturbing, and boomeranging to the individual as the self-source herself.

My mission is to have us enter spaces of fear-based habits that need to be opened to heartThinking possibilities provoking and engaging challenges to be taken. In other words, to drag the conscious along with the unconscious into meta-conscious realities. For example, most refuse to be engaged in past life's as influencing present life behaviors, but, overwhelmingly so, there is so much more, so let's try trans-WORDS as inducers of ShapeShifting realities for the emergence from the heart of compassion provoking birthing pains transcending the binary split-mind into radical new humane-human possibilities:

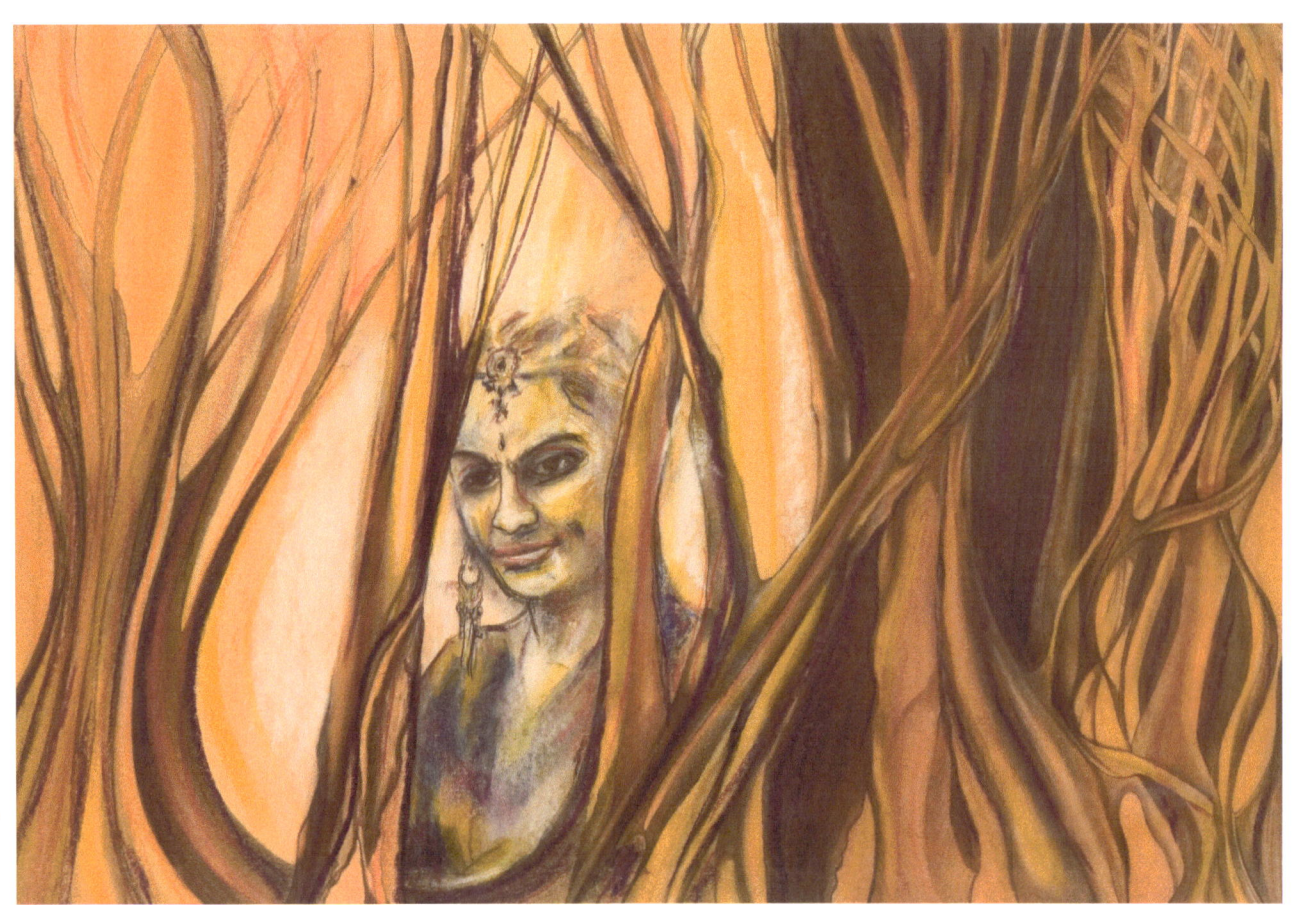

transmitting

transmutations

transitioning

transformations

transvestites

transsexuals

transliterations

transfigured

that is it

that is the way it is meant to be.

Intertwined with Nature

Conscious choices at specific universal
frequencies create space to be occupied,
and produce amazing, aware, and
predictable outcomes.

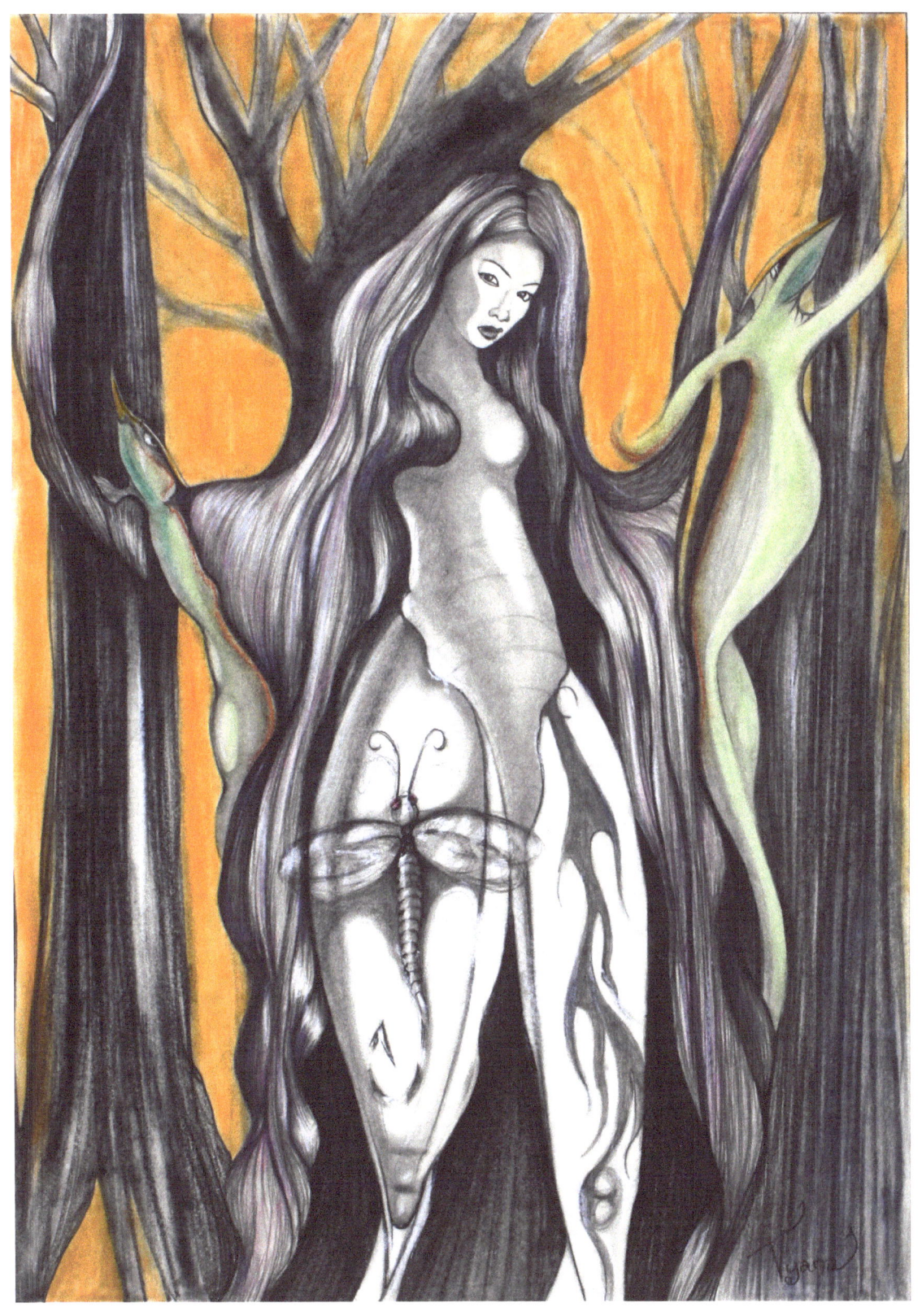

PART THREE

The Pain *of* Unrequited Love

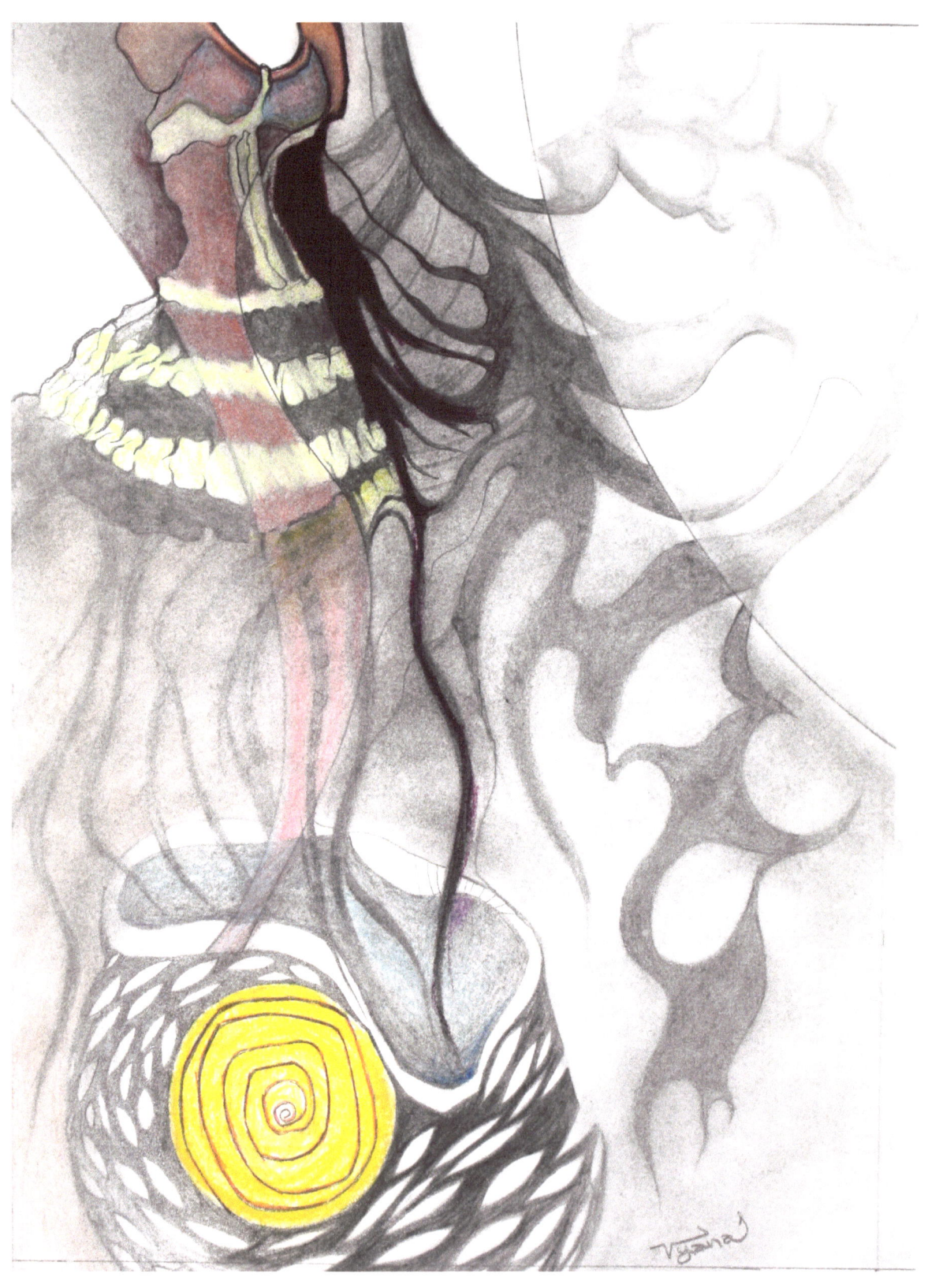

Unrequited Love: Bleeding Heart

Thinking of you, universal love,
my "spirit is dying."

"of love," you asked?

of crying birthings
of gentle dyings
of livings intended
of suicides contended
of vibrancy seen
of dull grey sicknesses
of bright red bleedings
of stitches meandering
of victories sudden
of lingering losses
of numbing indifference
of violence thwarted
of impositions proposed
of shielding barriers
of words unspoken
of words harshly spoken
of drenching in loathing
of swollen secrets
of surging assertions
of words whispered.

"of love," you asked?
of love I cannot tell you.

i can only tell you of my gifts.

falling down going up the stairs

1.
reversing perceptions
standing on heads
hanging upside down
sensing wanting partnership fulfilled
romantic and all.
yet, well, 'something' was not being real.

yes, desire was there
yet, my escape into you-there
for the possibility of completeness.
yet, all the while two persons incomplete
not a whole from 2 not whole!

2.
so i plunged in, ignoring my deep resonating
authenticity, my different and unique voice.
yet, wishing dearly for something that could not be.

impulsive madness overwhelming
rockBrain uprightWrongRight
continuously lost into 'impulsively-driven'
madness

3.
many years
ups and downs
downs and ups
always a gap
not of unkindness
but of invisible bridges not crossing
of intimacies not shared
a silence not of silence
a shiver, a not touch.
intentions not understood
momentum held back so sad
experienced as numbing indifference

4.
why did you not ask?
Were you as terrified as me to ask?
i was so very different than you thought i to be.
painfully you and i not hearing that which could not be!

yes, ultimately, i had to express me:
ALONE I WAS MEANT TO BE.

my notTruth with you, slaying me
and slaying you as well.

5.
years gone my now
i am FREE ALONE
but not with you.
i am so sorry that i had to be without you.
i was not fair to you and me!
i wished you well,
i did not mean to hurt you with:
i could only be what i must be.

all of those years falling down going up the stairs.
i could not find my feet
i had refused to acknowledge, to live, my heartVoice!!!

i thank you now for years ago.
in appreciation deep, i continue to wish you well.

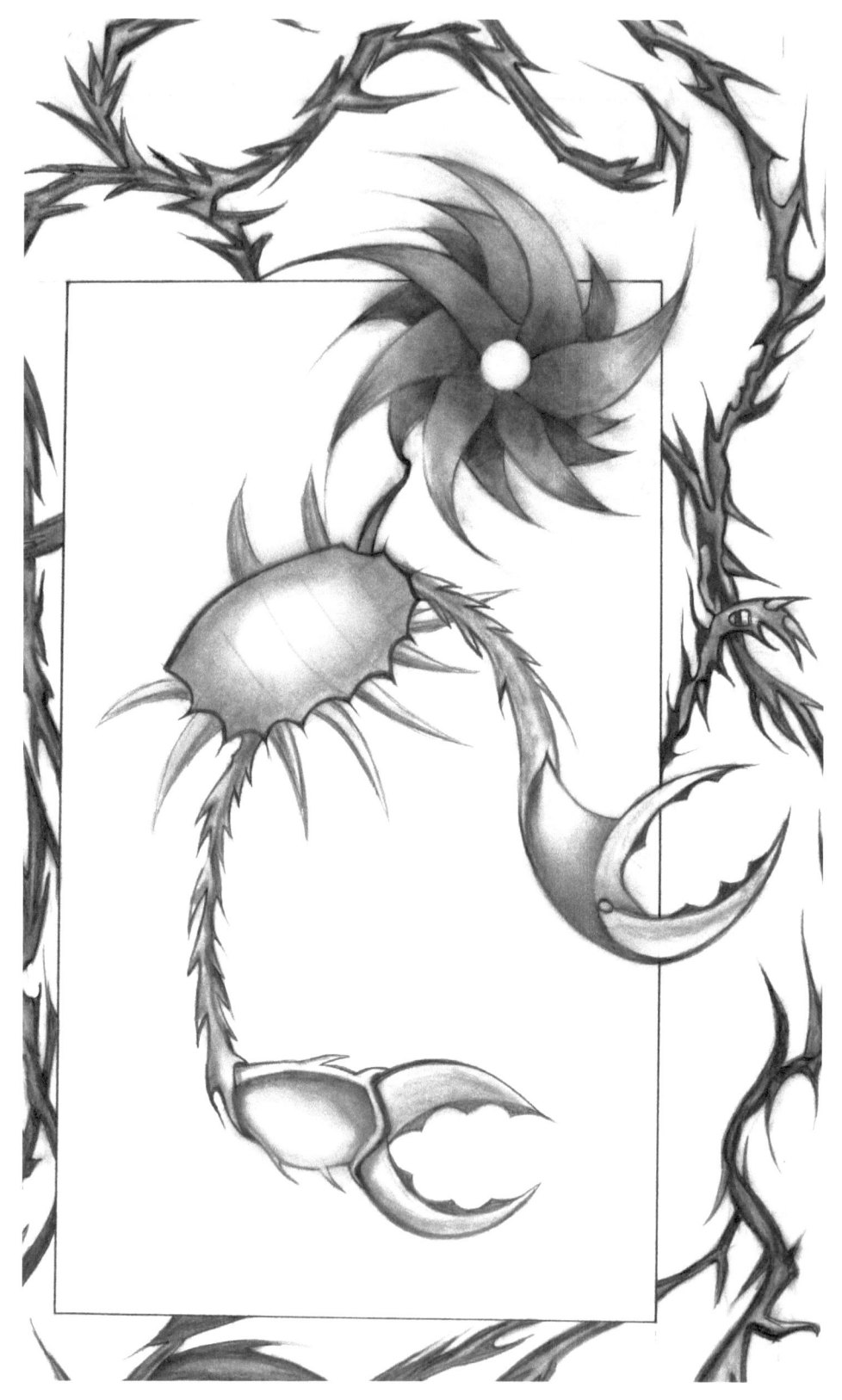

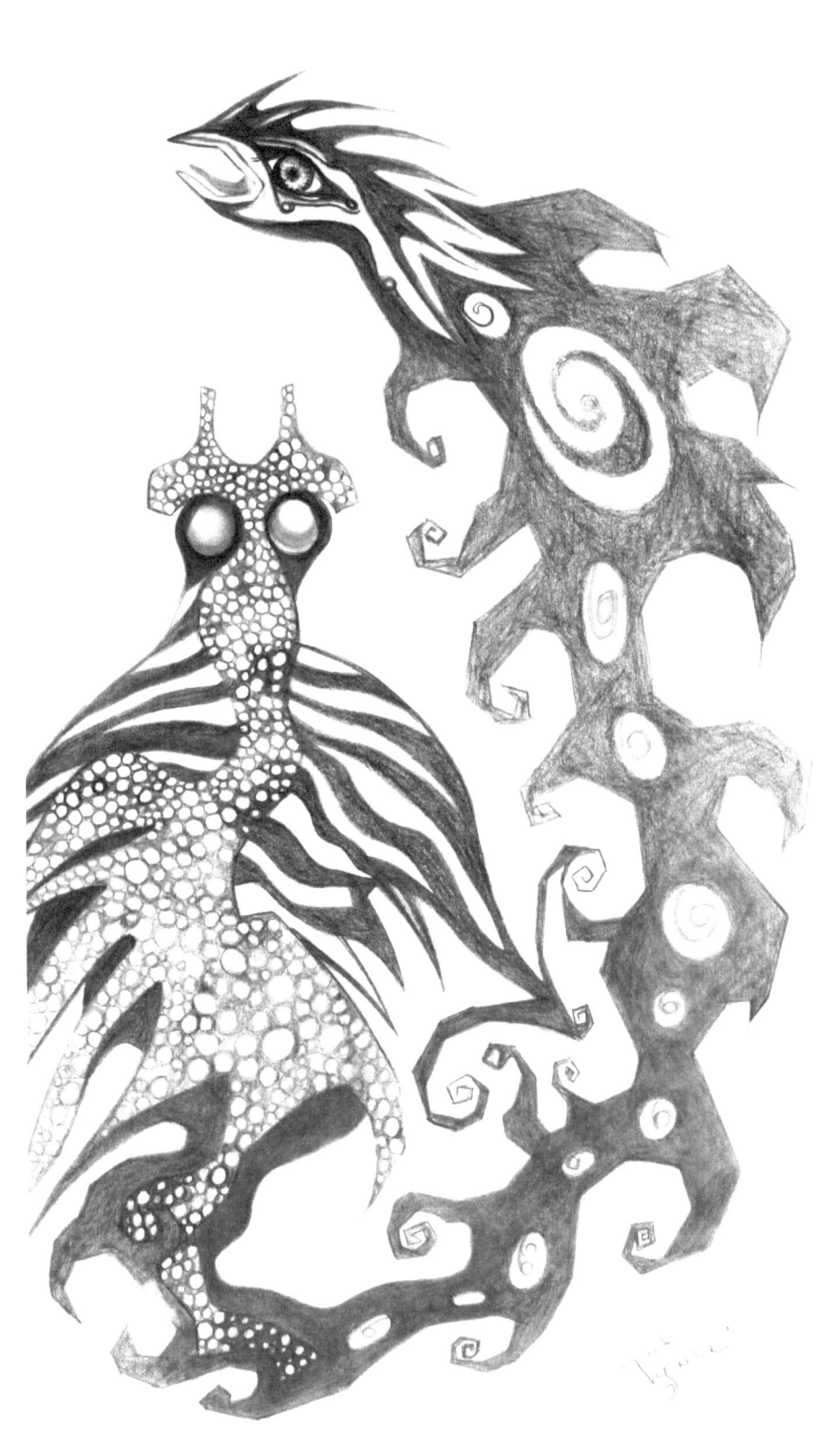

Embrace your Inner Self!

Opening the pearl of recognition:
member, dismember, and remember..

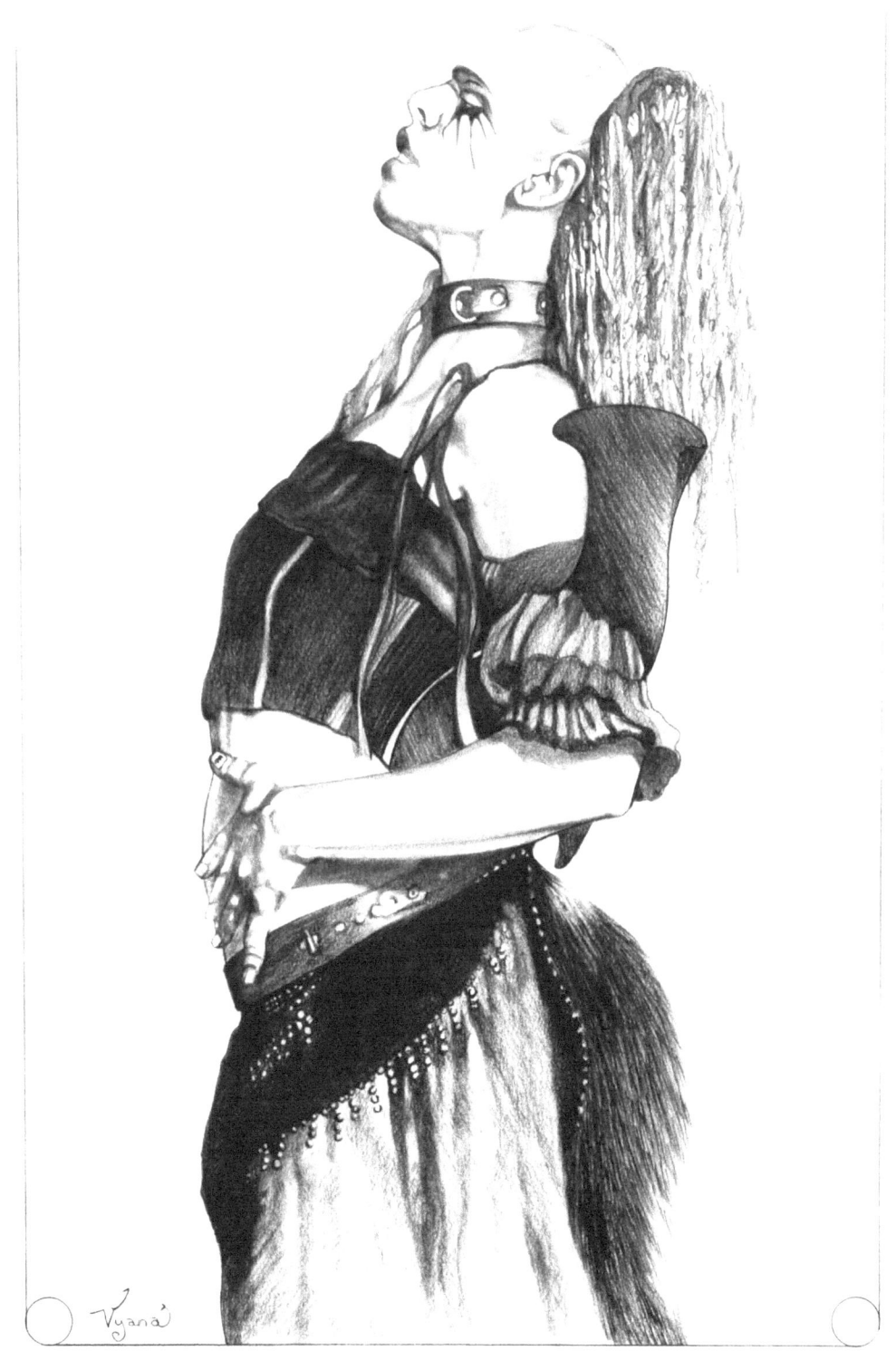

1"x 1," those eyes

1.
a pic, a photo, a 1 inch squared
those eyes that haunt
those eyes that i want to see into
those eyes

i linger
i look, and i pretend to not look at all
into those eyes that haunt me
those
eyes

i want to know of her mystery
i dare not ask as well
so i shall not ask
those eyes that haunt me
those eyes

2.
i am falling and falling into some well
yet, the well is only her deep dark eyes
that swell my eyes as well
i wonder about her sadness, and mine
i wonder about her happiness, and mine
in the darkness of her eyes
i wonder

i wonder about us dancing with the trees swaying
i wonder about the music that shall be played

and why this is meant to be
the way that it is meant to be

i linger and i wonder
for she is someone not contained.
i tremble and see in the stars
that she is so near, yet so far
unfathomable distances
yet not so far at all
as i tremble more

i look down and my forearm is there
yet, skin no more and i see my soul
coursing through my veins
and i wonder about her soul
so raw hidden behind those dark eyes once more
i wonder
i love

i see those dark eyes are love
and wonder

does she see me in the dark as well?
as i see her in the dark so well.

3.
i no longer have to wonder,
yet still full of wonder and awe
because all is love
love is love
love is
love

Bleeding Heart:
Yes, my drawingOut drawing

I have known you by many names,
and I have know you by no names.
and my heart has ached for you,
sweet One.

In a past life my heart truly exploded
and my blood drained from
my heart into my womb,
and, i could not find you,
and, my bird's nest
womb remained empty.
and, i remained without life.
and i lived in India,
and many other places as well.

you, sensitive One, are one of the *Ancient Ones*,
a so very precious one with a gentle and tender soul,
an ordinary-Xxtra-ordinary unique one,
and i know that you know that
and i know that you were born of FIRE

and i know that one time you were born
from the womb of my empty womb,
and not of water
but of FIRE
and, the evidence is
everywhere

i knew you then as a primal scream
i know you now as my primal scream
you awakening me to your presence,
you being one of the Ancient Ones.

I also see-saw you as giving
breath to me
birth to me
i cried then.
i cry now.

please write to me
and tell me of your FIRE
please write to me

and tell of your beauty,
which cannot be contained.

please tell me how your voice
has become the voice of me
please tell me about the
voice of our ancient ancestors.
please tell of your beauty
your love
and why i see you
and why i was not able to find the
soul of you
hidden from me for so long.

please tell of your secrets
please tell me of your wisdom
please tell me why you cry
please tell of what you have known
please tell me of what you have lost
please tell me about love.

i linger by the side of the pond
as i await the breath of you
as i await the soul of you.
i know if i am quiet i will hear you.
i know if i am very still,
i will see you
waiting by the edge of the pond
waiting
waiting

no longer waiting
i love you

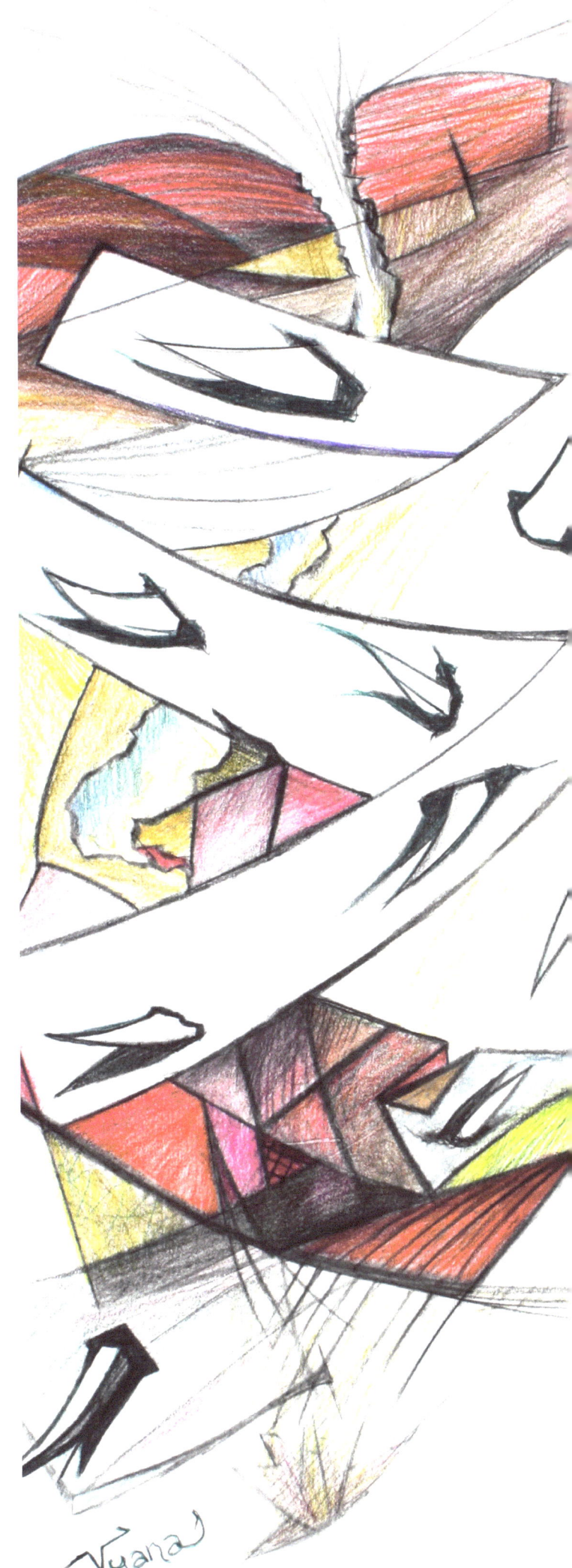

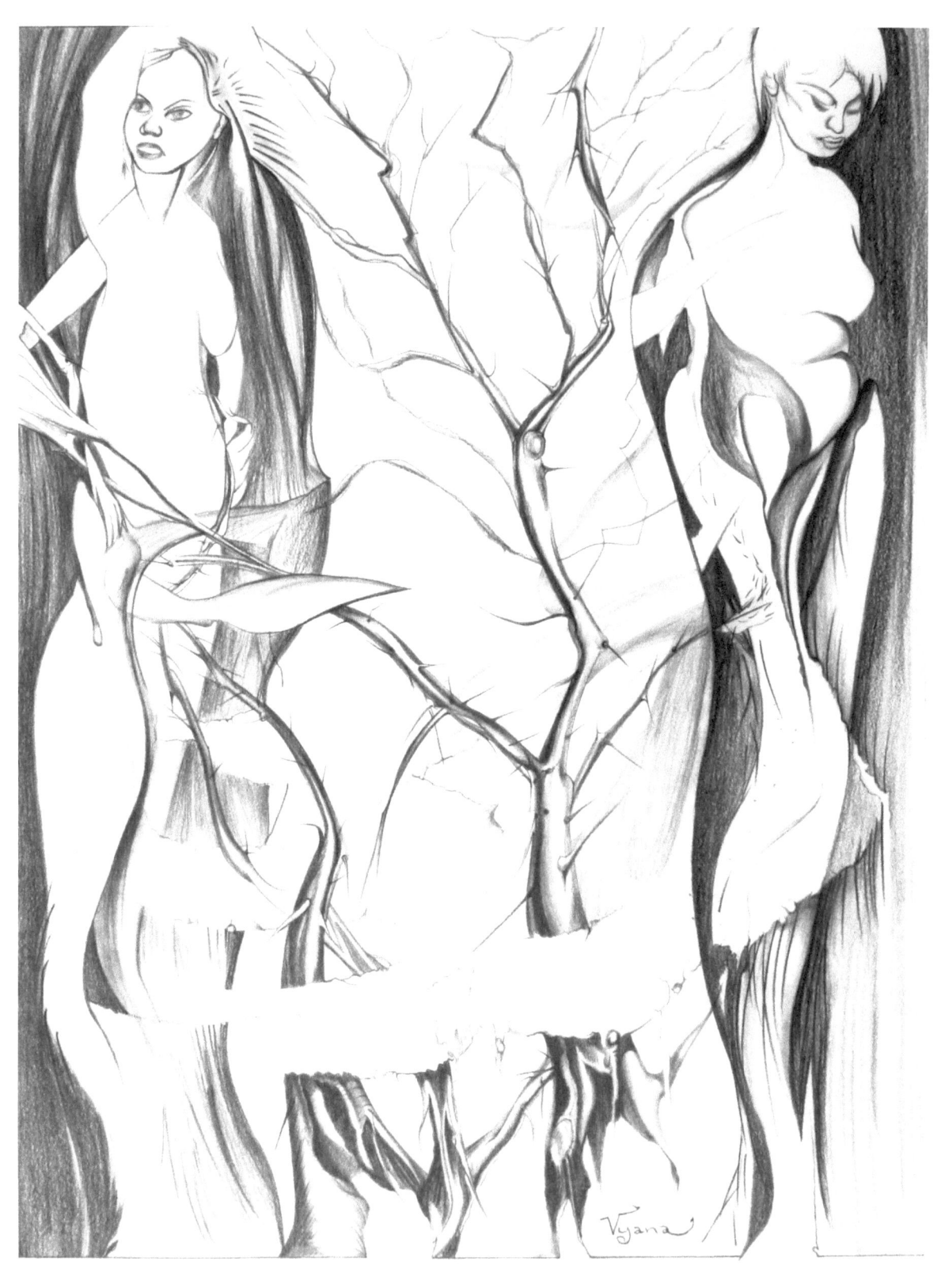

Severed at it's "roots,"
love is Killed.

love hurts

love hurts
i cannot explain it in any other way
every time i go out into the world
i do not, have not, ever been able to deal with love:
a lost soul am I
have i ever been able to love

How would i know?

love is so much suffering,
and that is not what i want
and since that is so,
as everyone i know is suffering in some way
i cannot tolerate suffering anymore
i feel like i am dying today.

so, how can i write?
there is no destiny here, only fate
there seems to be only suffering in what i am living
for it imprisons me into chambers with
sleepless nights
turmoil
shame
and
ruminations

i have lost my way
and i never want to return home again.

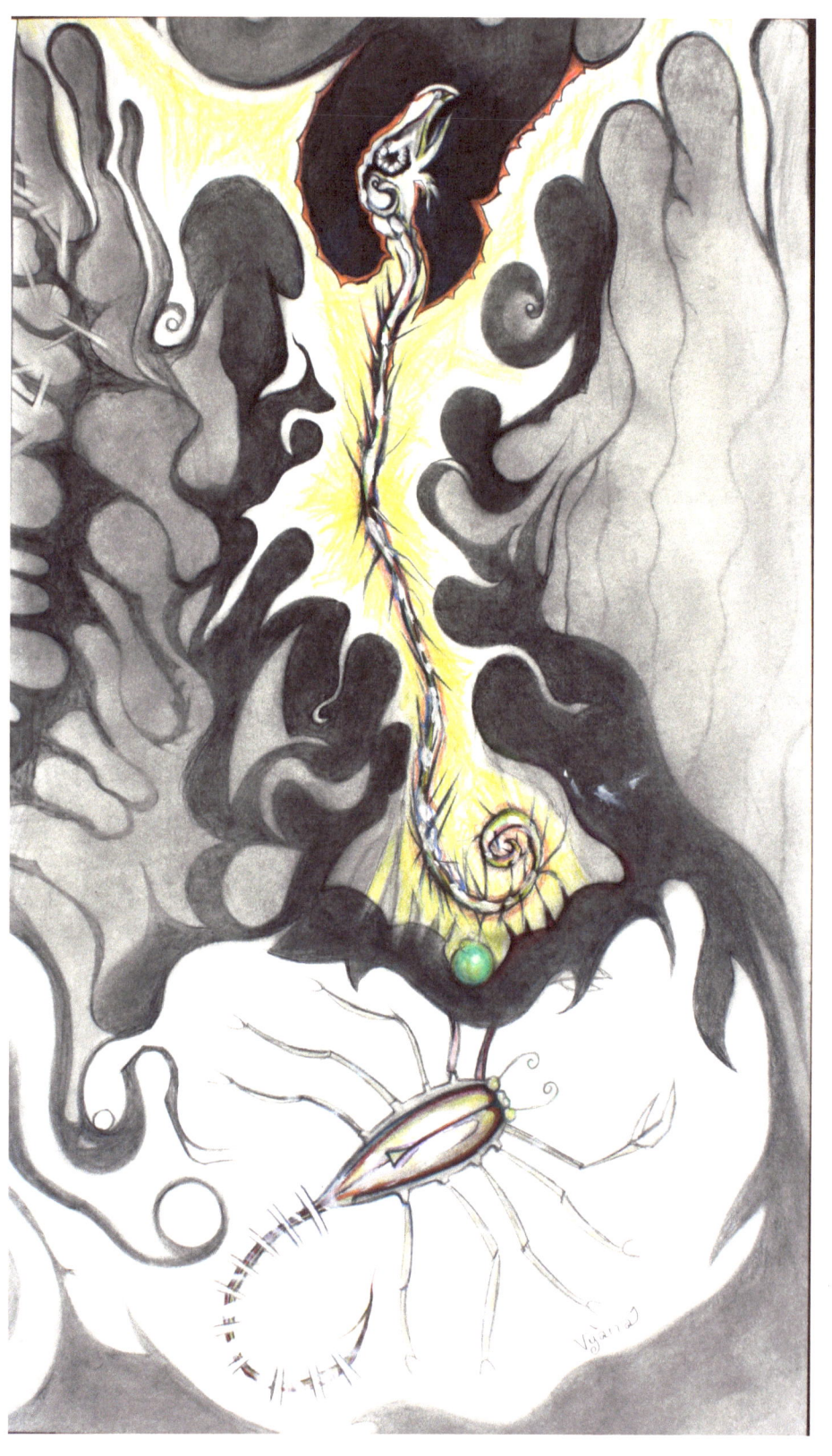

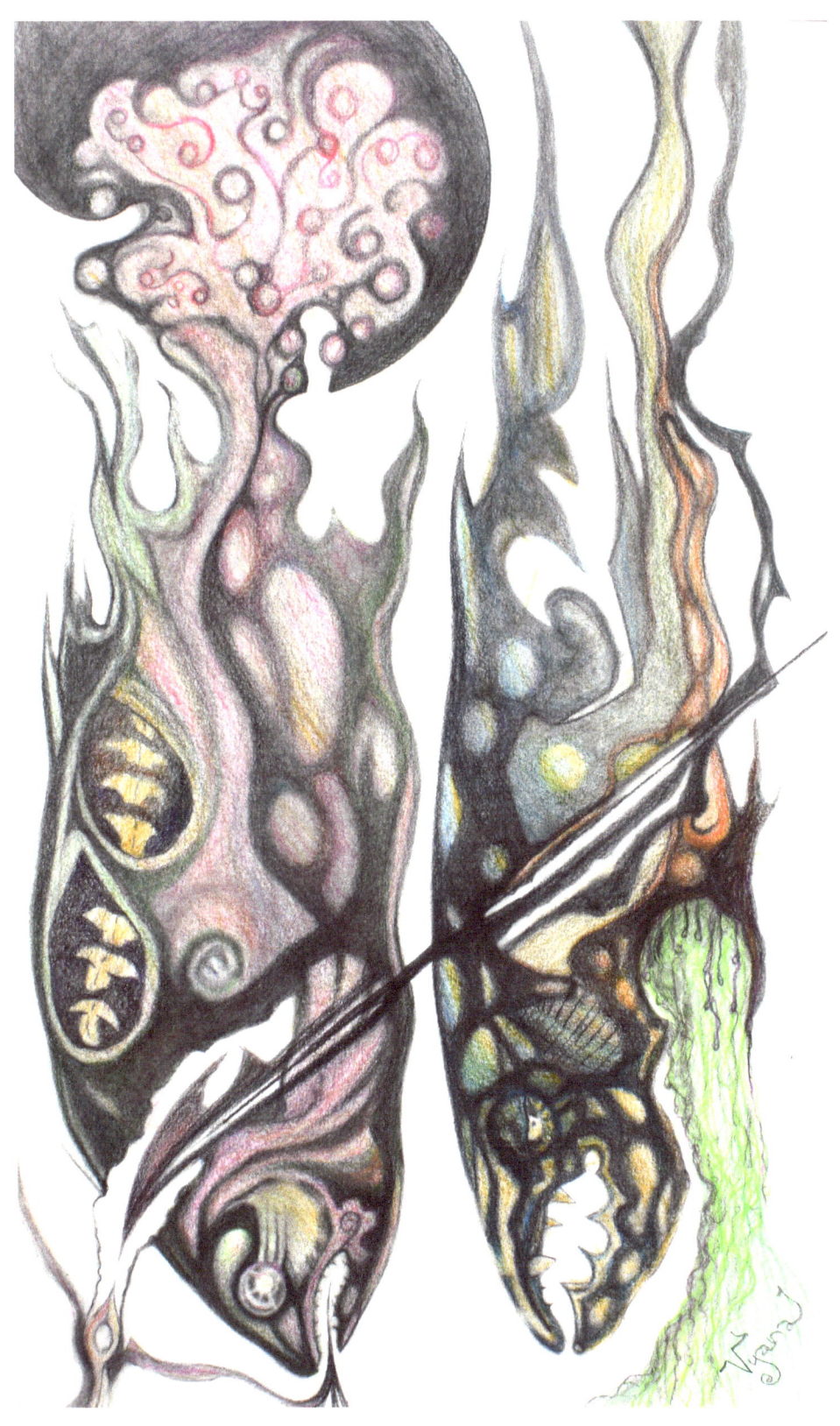

sensing you

1.
raining today, crying today!
many passing-through thoughts today
an un-suppressed i am,
and you are!

raining stopping
sunsetting
A melancholy mood coming over me
in the form of a beautiful
sweet
sadness
sublime and precious
surely that is you!

2.
I, taking my chance today
... life is fragile.
childishly out-of-control romantics we/us
indulging those sweet dreams
guiding us, revealing us.

yet, sometimes it is best to
look the other way!
probably done writing these poems
too fragile for me
eye shall see at
sunshining
lots of love

PART FOUR

The Eight Day
Poem

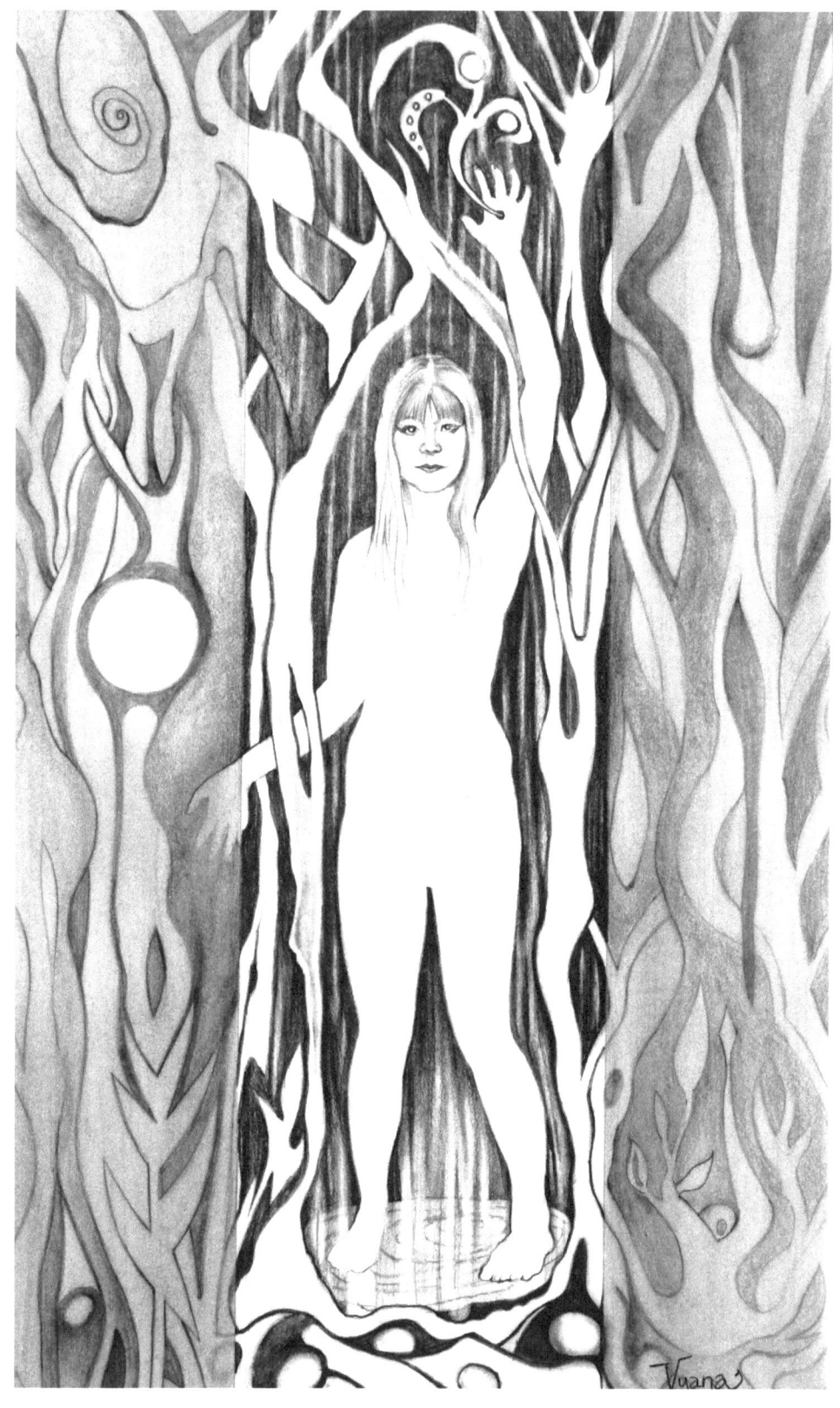

Day 1

somewhere along the way

1 ... abandoning me ...

my calling has become stranger in recent years—no end to this opening intensity—absorbing coming through me clear through conversations meeting only with sameness, not of a calling.

NO TEASING, How will i learn if i do not ask?

INNOCENT me, I think i am aware, YET, there is a me that has not been integrated, for i see I HAVE FOUR HEARTS, because the heart has four chambers. YET, NOT READY for something is ASKING OF ME to pay attention to ME, my inner self, yet ABANDONED THROUGH CONDITIONING TO HIDE my own heart, and, in a moment, flash, i now am returning backwards as i am MY THREE YEAR OLD SELF speaking to me now:

you, the innocent One going out into the World — with many moments to learn about self, when, yet, I PROTEST, i am not there outside in that world, because i am from INSIDE the world, MY world. So, now, i see i that am FORCING MYSELF to find compassion, and was informed by the multitudes not to ask for feedback or to really feel directly my own hearts ... sadness PREVAILS FOR A LIFETIME it seems!!!

however, there is a message within this message from ME-TO-ME receiving between my own four hearts denied by external pleasing, and this me-to-me is calling back to me penetrating my own 4hearts: what has not been received ... SCARED / FEARFUL ... an opening ... lackingUnconditional love i am now EXPOSED.

so, my INNER VOICE says: What will happen if i STOP feeling, worrying, and planning?
Thus, i SINK taking me deeper into DISCOMFORT deeper now, and i ask again: What will i be experiencing when i stop feeling? What will happen if i stop planning?

What will happen if i were to NOT STOP, AND SINKING, sinking deeper now...

and, the voice says: whatever emerges, you want to accept because what is happening in you is: YOU DEFENDING YOU. so, the inner voice tells me to BE EXCEEDINGLY GENTLE and CALL THIS MESSAGE FORWARD. BE VERY GENTLE as if it were a parents voice speaking to a child!!!!!

Sensing, feeling, ultra sensitive, it is okay that 'it' is here, but it does NOT seem that way at all, does it?

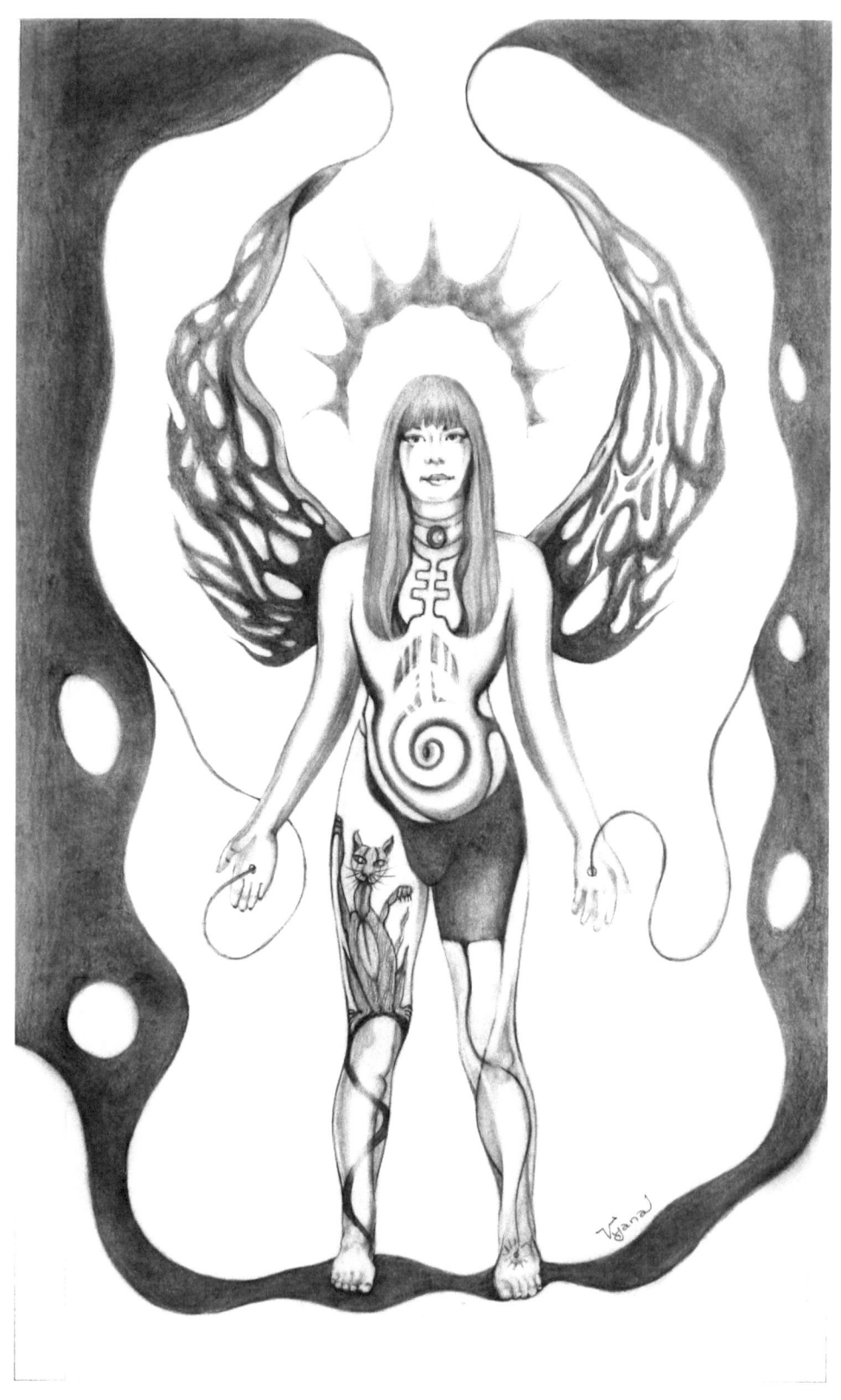

Day 2

somewhere along the way

2 ... abandoning destiny ... !!!

destiny dial into my belly,

and dial down my mind,

for trust has abandoned me

RAW ENERGY MYSTERY call it forward the self-preservation those parts of me, abandoned: let it unwind and give attention to self my

CONFRONTATION WITH WORTH, yet love calls you back pondering to YOU, and....adrenaline running as not safe abandoned, SO FEAR IS SAFE, as feared sensations in my belly, where nothing is safe, not safe, not safe.

gritty, but does not bulldoze me pushing ... PUSH INSIDE RESPONSES, i am existing in two worldsSPLITworlds, yet have not done anything wrong, but

SHAME

is a BIG picture very personal, and impersonal, although developed capacities deep questioning still now questioning self-intimacy.

ASKING AND SEEKING me a gentle compassionate loving self pondering being lost with self

longing for ... feedback: Something is calling me to be clear, to be closer — so TRUST can emerge, for what is opening is me???

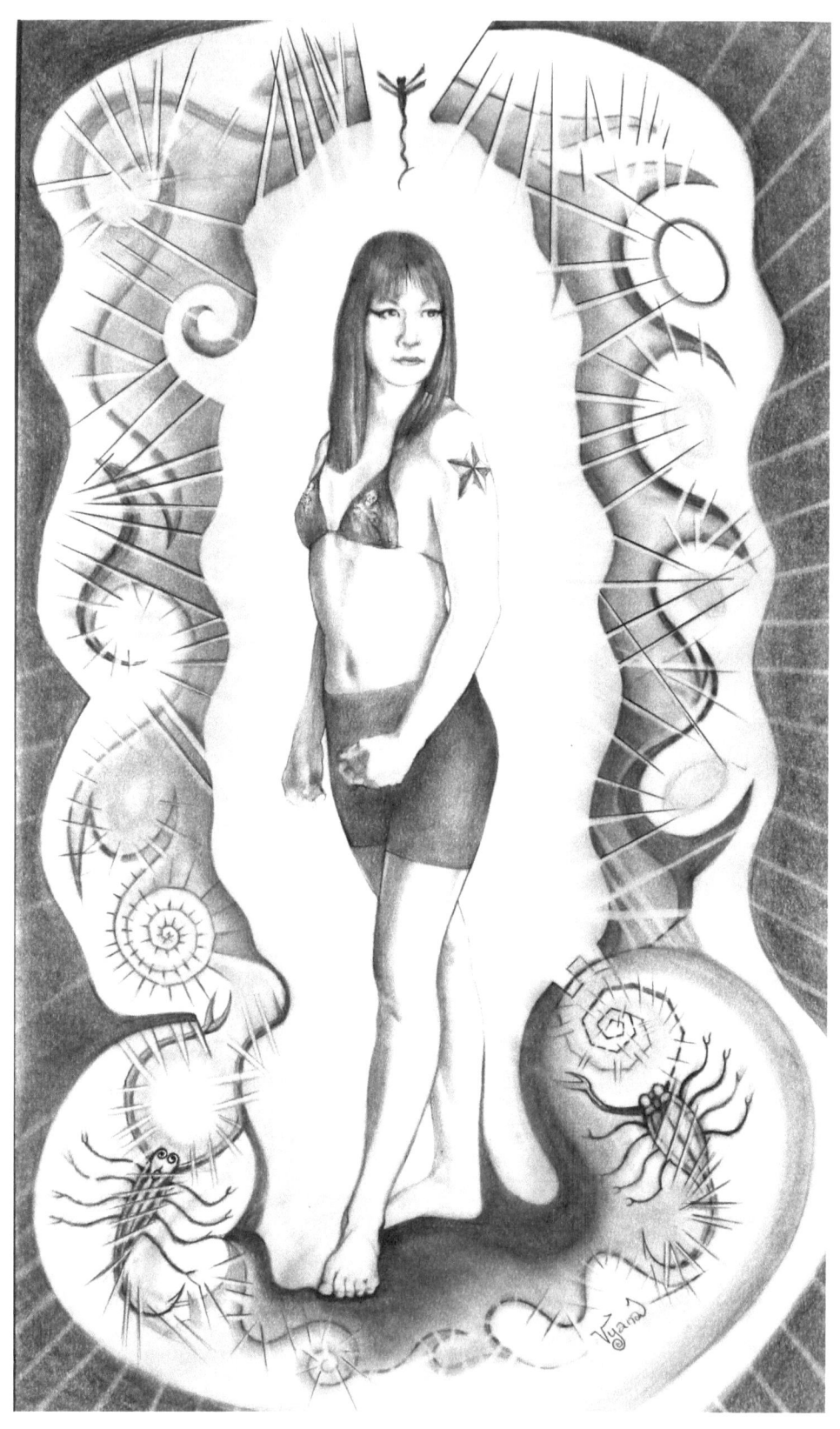

Day 3

somewhere along the way

3 ... urgency ... !!!

longing to express
meaningful expression
urgency arises???
yes, always there
motivating, and frustrating my energy field
as urgency overwhelms me-and-me
maybe trusting what is opening, ok?
'drawing into' that experience of me
there is a 'drawing out' you could say.
What am i feeling when i 'draw into' me?
nurturance for what?
for nurturing me-as-me?
a deeper calling, an innate longing?
satisfaction as sacred longing?
feeling disembodied as not trackable,
i seek deeper body nuances
going deeper by turning into
very immediate experiential
body sensations
observing, not thinking
observing, not judging
lingering
pondering 'feeling-words' arising into awareness
sensitive
responding
listening to that longing,
but, contradiction is teacher in me as going outwards,
distracting me-from-me
yet, always, inherently real
right herethere inside of me.
be soft as strong
be gentle
be there

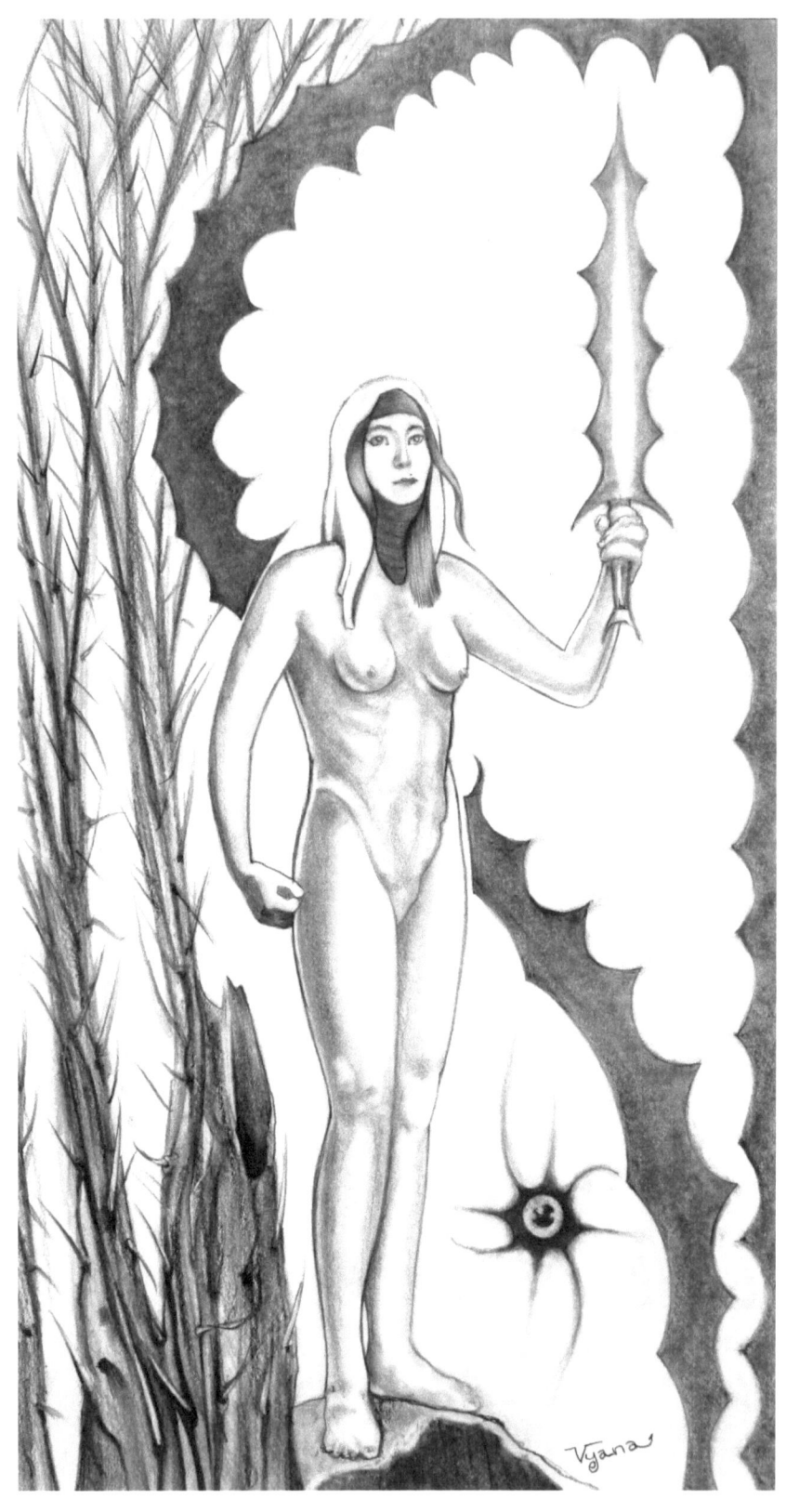

Day 4

somewhere along the way

4 … meSHAMEdagger … !!!

core-WOUND in my body, and no place else.....constructing an identity, and rattles my construction.......and, i am obsessed when i cannot feel, because mental FeelsNOT. feel what body? where is it in me? to dismantle it is to find the REAL AS REAL goes into me; lives in my body:

ENCOUNTER with my BODY

immediate response is it grabs at me; really the mind grabs at me. but do not allow mind to SHAME it = do not shame it. CREATE = pay attention:

fast track

infinite patience … QUALITY INVITES it in even though it is shame … must turn towards it because it does not know itself:

complete change, tears flow / TEARS FLOW / tears flow

at these parts of me left out in the cold, and

they open up to me!!

feedback critical towards NOT IN control telling me, "It is okay!!!"

say it is okay, Okay?

triggers my own pain … triggers me … meSHAMEdagger

who in my life not caring avoidance of feeling into TERROR-REAL

overcompensating energy using dispersing

MOVING willingly NOW to MEET THE PAINavoidance

free in Xpression do not need validation

tears flow … tears flow … tears flow

fear sends out of my body

 … softening the landing

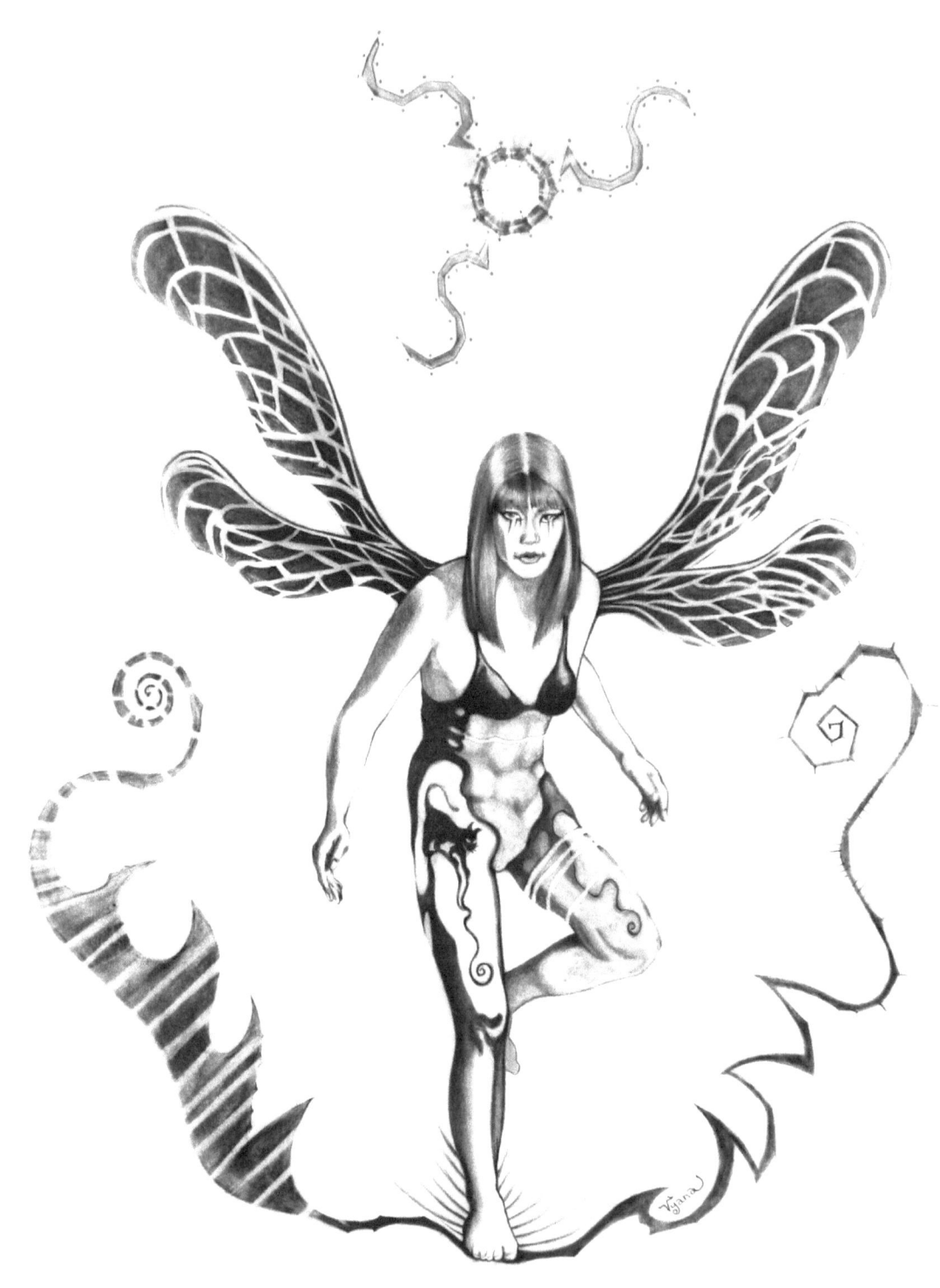

Day 5

somewhere along the way

5 ... calling your presence ... !!!

sitting in stillness: Stop!!! experience it ... non-doing. What? let pain be ... you are okay inside not to be fluent as defensive blocks flip-out/flip-in ... Safe Self ... liberation InSide as tired of those old stories ... Love this? Challenge Questions!!! Space? find out more!!!

no way protests!!!

Calling your presence, expands capacity!!!

turning hardened Wall of Protection efficient

always in the body

mind defenses separate from heart underneath

being so strong is not good or bad

calm in crises!!!

how to respond to own woundedness would be addressed to my presence

absorbing negative energies 2 functions: being there through someone else, or heart2heart, which is startling because heart2heart changes other people ... do not need to work so hard at it any more.

quality = quality of my experience of how my eyes open in the moment, rather than expectations of how to be, and not dropping into the contrived reality of the identity

dropping further into what is here = tune into that

For example: agitation at 4 a.m. — find out what was herethere.

Ok, i am here — changing my own system talking to the agitation

really need

to go

deeper

how to be with the angst in a loving way

listening, turning outward not a true place,

the wheel of honesty ... have to be safe

practical way — recognize — notice — allow it be herethere:

What do i need?

ATTENTION

AFFECTION

APPRECIATION

ACCEPTANCE

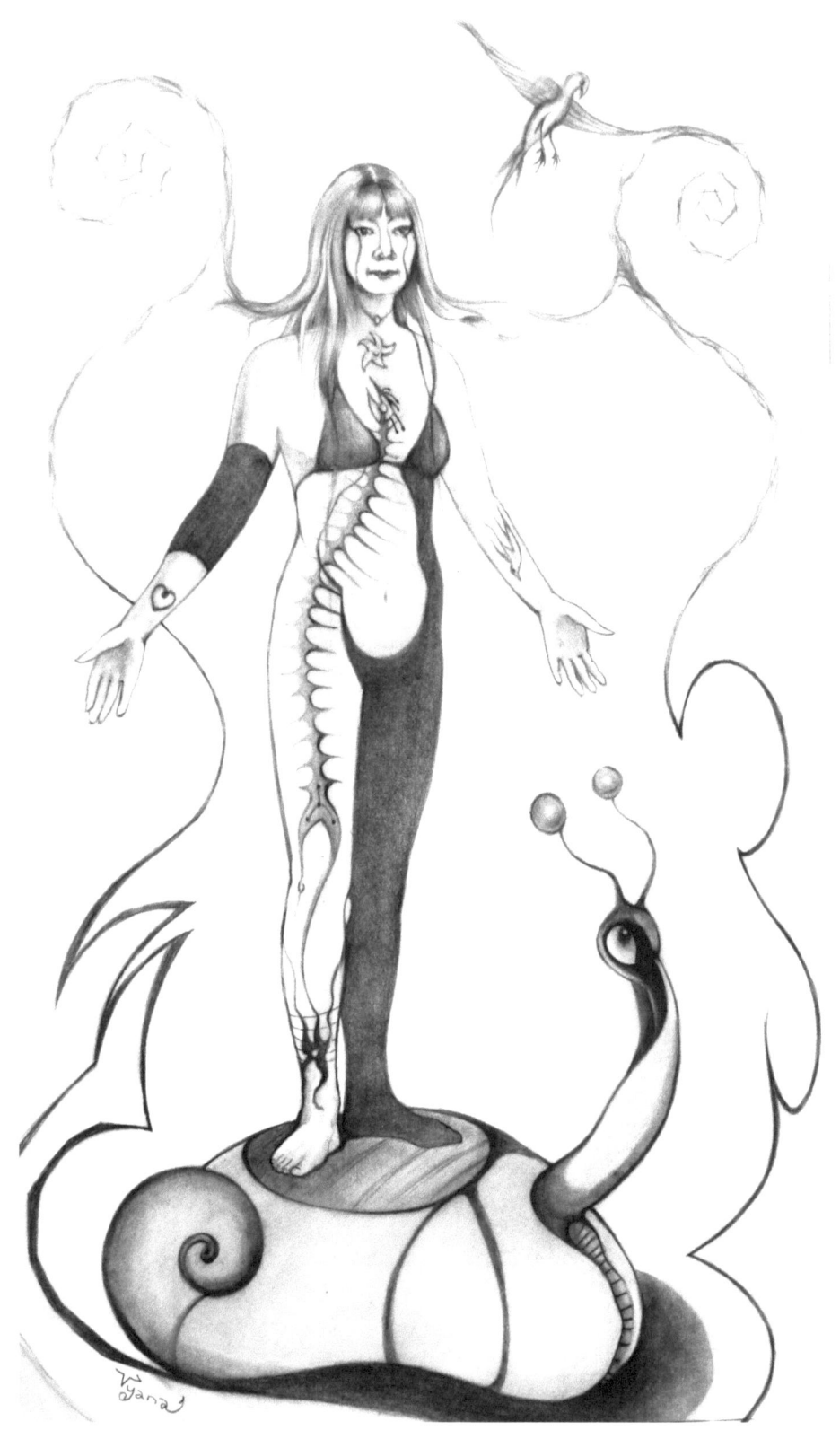

Day 6

somewhere along the way

6 … tears softening … !!!

sense of urgency too prevalent like an engine idling inside of me, so be curious. what is the energy behind this urgency? what questions need to be asked? what is a scene like where this occurs?

Oh, yes, that old issue: identifying with survival.

identity is being kept underneath so powerless

wounded? not enough?

false antidote is to turn forward

avoidance of pain and self-love and self-caring

so curious i am overcompensating afraid of what is going to fail

worse case scenario feeling in my body?

LOOK INTO so not avoiding = overcompensating = more hurt and

no ease in body

STOP = do not focus on changing outcomes, INCREDIBLE, a profound feeling that unsuccessful is ok becomes a desire for an 'about face.'

What is hurting here?

Be CURIOUS!!!

all entanging mess relationship with myself

READY, or not? = hiding me = STOP avoidance survival overcompensating

path of compassion = a softening into the body into the energy field elicits

readiness to compassion as it is natural spaceCOMPASSION becomes recognized as True Compassion!!!!!!!!!!!!!

identity falsely tell untruths so as to think i do not appreciate me, and, an inner voice screams:

DO NOT BECOME SOMETHING THAT YOU ARE NOT

the longing resumes from previous days

in contrast to self as identity so i can open inside

RESPONSE to longing resumes:

how did i construct my identity?

how can i stop my identity?

Ok, it is a process, right?

Tears softening me into being only a patient HEART softening softening tears flowing

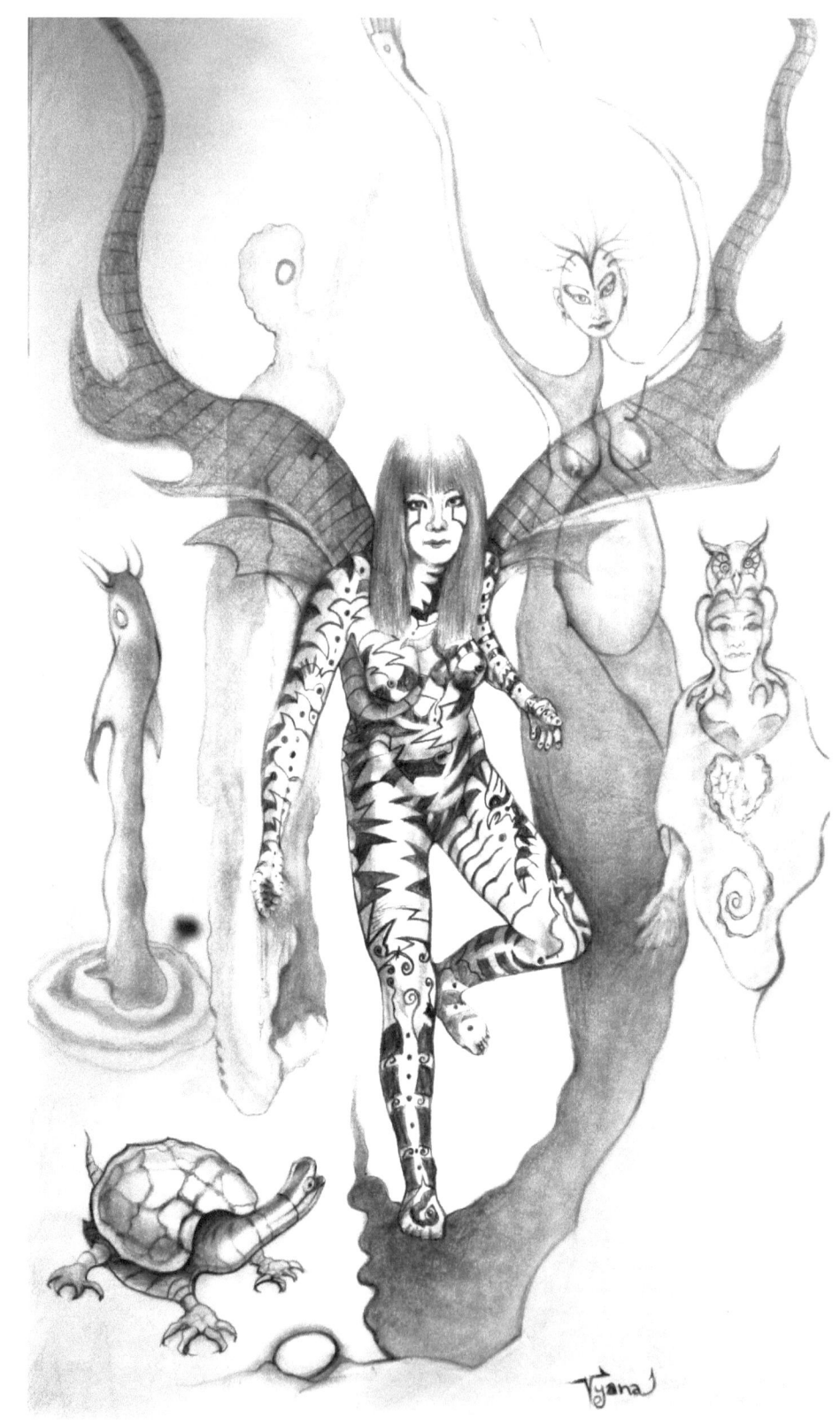

Day 7

somewhere along the way

7 ... the circle was broken ... !!!

cannot decipher — endless frustration for me — my hyper-senstitivity does not help as i lose myself, but actually that is Self, just challenging to deal with me at times.

so my 'losing self' chart would be a circle representing my CORE FEELINGS SPACE CENTER: feelings, angst, and feedback, and the outer 7 modalities are too terrifying that i choose not to express presently, for i think they will break me, vulnerability much, and that saddens me!

however, be curious: a KNOT CAN BE UNRAVELED: breathingHEART in-BREATH LOVE ENTERS, and on exhalation RELAX, and notice our conditioning moves each of us away from ourHEART as my life: did not get help, a mentor, a confidant, yet still drawn to restingHEART. Did not Get? did not get, yet i have the priority of the FEEDBACK LOOP, which disturbs me so, when not herethere....waiting, waiting fb frustrates even more ... teaching is outward, so i even dread outward and angst sets in ... in ... in ...

what is the validation of, Who i am? my secretive personality blocks sense of not working, fear of merging - cannot merge - afraid of?

what happens when 'not existing?'

what happens when 'not visible?'

resolution possible: mining deeply into its impetus - see the contradiction, the introversion and not being visible, yet wanting visibility ... when lackingFEEDBACK LOOP HURTS?? LIBERATING FROM THE PAIN? Open? it is actually natural the 'play of opposites!!!!!!!!!!!!!!!!!!!!!!!!' this makes me even more curious, so i become even more curious — as there is something NOT WRONG IN ME — so, by being RESOLUTE i one can resolve!!!

be RESOLUTE now: it hurts, yes, but 'mine' it, and let it open and inform me = backing off, and i am feeling lighter ... and it allows the SPACE TO OPEN as the now notCONTRACTION issue has merely been stuck in my own belief system thinking i am not lovable, so where do i go to find LIVING IN LIVING??????????????????

all-in-BODY is true, so approach with love and compassion, the sacred vessel of your/our/my being ... soften/soften space as old 'wound arises,' and it is in space ... ACKNOWLEDGE ITS EXISTENCE

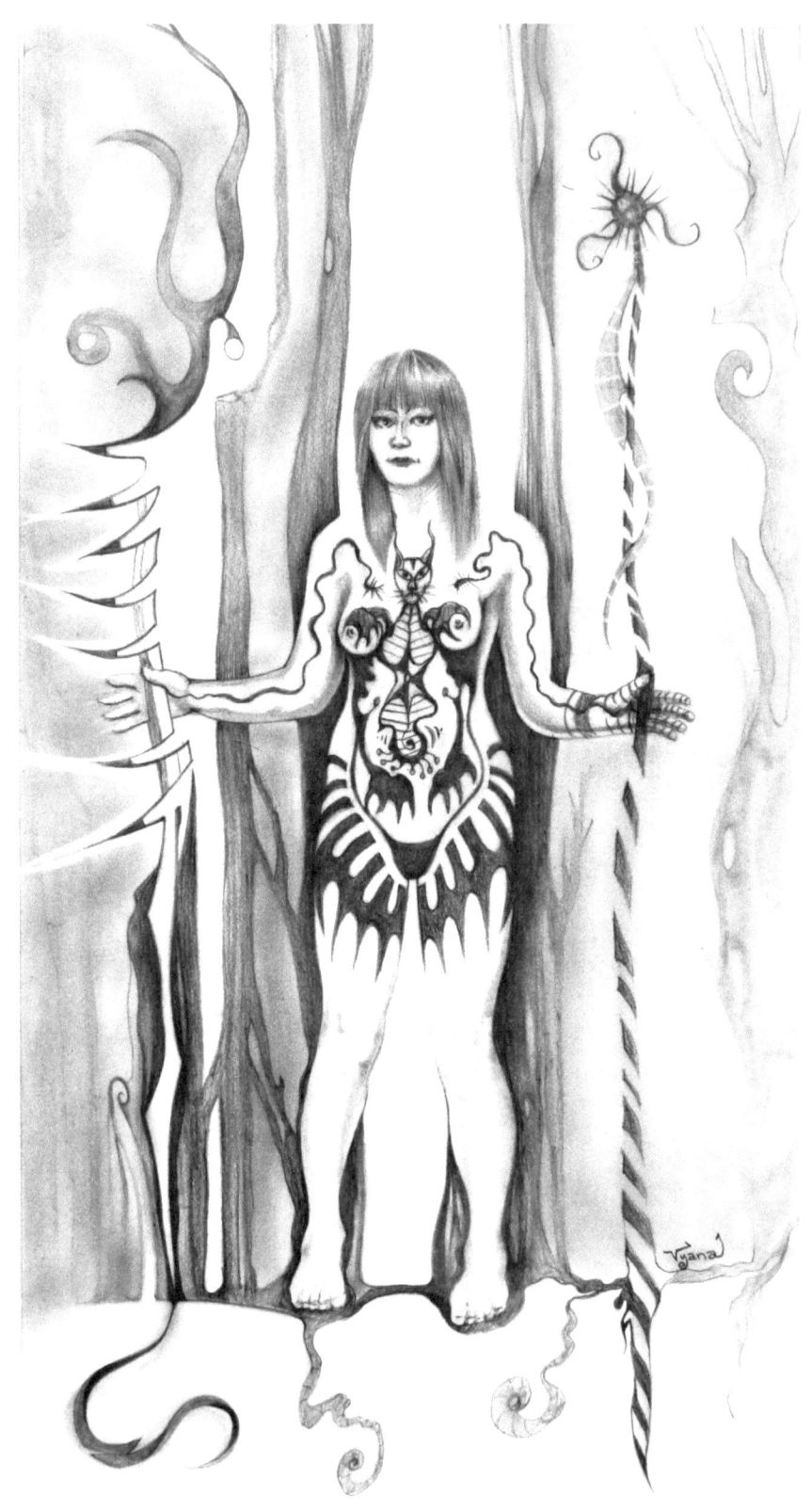

Day 8

somewhere along the way

8 ... i was born into a whirlwind ...

so many events and 1000s of thoughts and feelings make up a lifetime, and, insights can give us access to our pain, and our joy in life. However, the EGO just seems to go on compensating for my/our inadequacies: there seems to be a system that the EGO has to dupe us over and over again.

so, it is a certain QUALITY OF EXPRESSION, THINKING, AND FEELING that i need to bring to what was hurting in me, me in the world; and, my COMMITMENT TO PURSUE ME.

a HEART not tended to always goes outward to look for love, and seeks an interaction, a FEEDBACK to quiet things down, be happy, and find satisfaction.

so, the nature of RELATIONSHIPS to self and others are helpful to appease some of the pain of living, especially creatively.

if only outward one will hit a wall, and that will force one back into oneself, and this is interesting because it is a circle both outward and inward that is the source of TRUE LOVE.

it really is 1 + 1 = 1, and in that dualism transcending into 1, One [oneness] there is a peace and contentment that can be vitally alive inside, and in relationship to another, to others, to the world, to the Universe.

so, how do we do this, ie, what is the PROCESS, if words, or being ONLY outside or inside are not going to take us to our essence?

it begins with a QUALITY OF TENDERNESS

it begins with a QUALITY OF FRIENDSHIP

meaning it begins in my/our energy fields where INTENTION IS PLACED.

SO, then what happens with inadequacy?

well, first the ego is constricted like a KNOT in the solar plexus

well, then there are images not of peace

well, then we begin to RECOGNIZE we have been conditioned extensively.

all of our lives

well, so SUCCESS, generally means you stand ALONE-lonely!!!!!!!

so, de-conditioning is a terrible process because you come to realize that there is tremendous pain inside there disturbing you, and it is not a fleeting sensation; it seems it will never go away.

so, finally 'de-conditioning' cracks one open and forces one to look inward.

here is what i found in this inward looking:

teach from the heart

life is calling continuously to find the callingHEARTcalling YOU

it can be complicated the way this CALLING SPEAKS to YOU

it can induce even more anxiety, and you finally ask,

How can i continue to be with this anxiety, this angst, this omission???

Here is what i learned as well: be a FRIEND TO YOURSELF, EACH ONE OF US the best we can, and CULTIVATE that self-FRIENDSHIP.

FINALLY, we/us begin to TRANSCEND IDENTITY!!!!!!

love is

but, even then, this friendship can be without a DESTINATION as we will not be familiar to being with Self-in-LIFE.

so, to be LOVE on this journey is to begin to remove the layers blocking love, and the tricky part is, if done with the EGO one can never be satisfied.

so, here is the rudimentary structure of OUR PROCESS PLAN:

1. RECOGNIZE what triggers non-compassionate reactions. you may even have a panic attack realizing these triggers are defined by ego.

2. ALLOW: everything that we do has a PHYSIOLOGICAL CONTEXT, yet we mistakenly think that it is mind that gives context. however, LOGIC is notCONSCIOUSNESS because then our ENERGY WILL BE DIFFUSED.

3. therefore, we need to TEND THROUGH INQUIRY, a PAYING ATTENTION that allows each of us to deal with What does the ego want? repeating, What does the ego want from me??? What does my EGO-NEED FROM ME? well, it certainly does not want you to lose your INVENTED IDENTITY!!!

so, it becomes necessary to dissolve the ego, to transmute the energy into our own bodies so as to create a real and visible difference in how our BODY APPEARS, that is, EXPRESSES ITSELF INTO THE WORLD. therefore, I perceive that we have an INHERENT RESPONSIBILITY TO OWN UP TO WHAT WE ARE GIVING [?] TO THE WORLD as we are perceived. yes, it is OUR RESPONSIBILITY.

4. REST: every time we/us go through this process, the BODY NEEDS REST in order to re-fuel and re-balance the ENERGY SYSTEMS of the body = being in the BODY FULLY ... breathing is spirit that connects, that bridges, the inner and outer worlds, and it is the only process in human anatomy that does this, thus, it is our IMPERATIVE to be aware and use this process.

finally, THE BODY OPENS NOT AS A THING, BUT AS A SACRED LIVINGLOVINGLIVING PROCESS OF TRANSMUTATION of non-awareness FULLY INTO CONSCIOUS COMPASSION.

TO SUMMARIZE:

1. RECOGNIZE & notice compassionately.

2. ALLOW the body to be in context in all micro-macro levels in the Universe.

3. TEND TO, dissolve, and transmute.

4. REST

we can then NEUTRALIZE quickly because it is a NATURAL WAY = a NEW WAY OF BEING = NO wars, no analysis as the logical mind can take a break ... this gives YOUR LIFE CONTEXT = it MAKES SENSE!!!

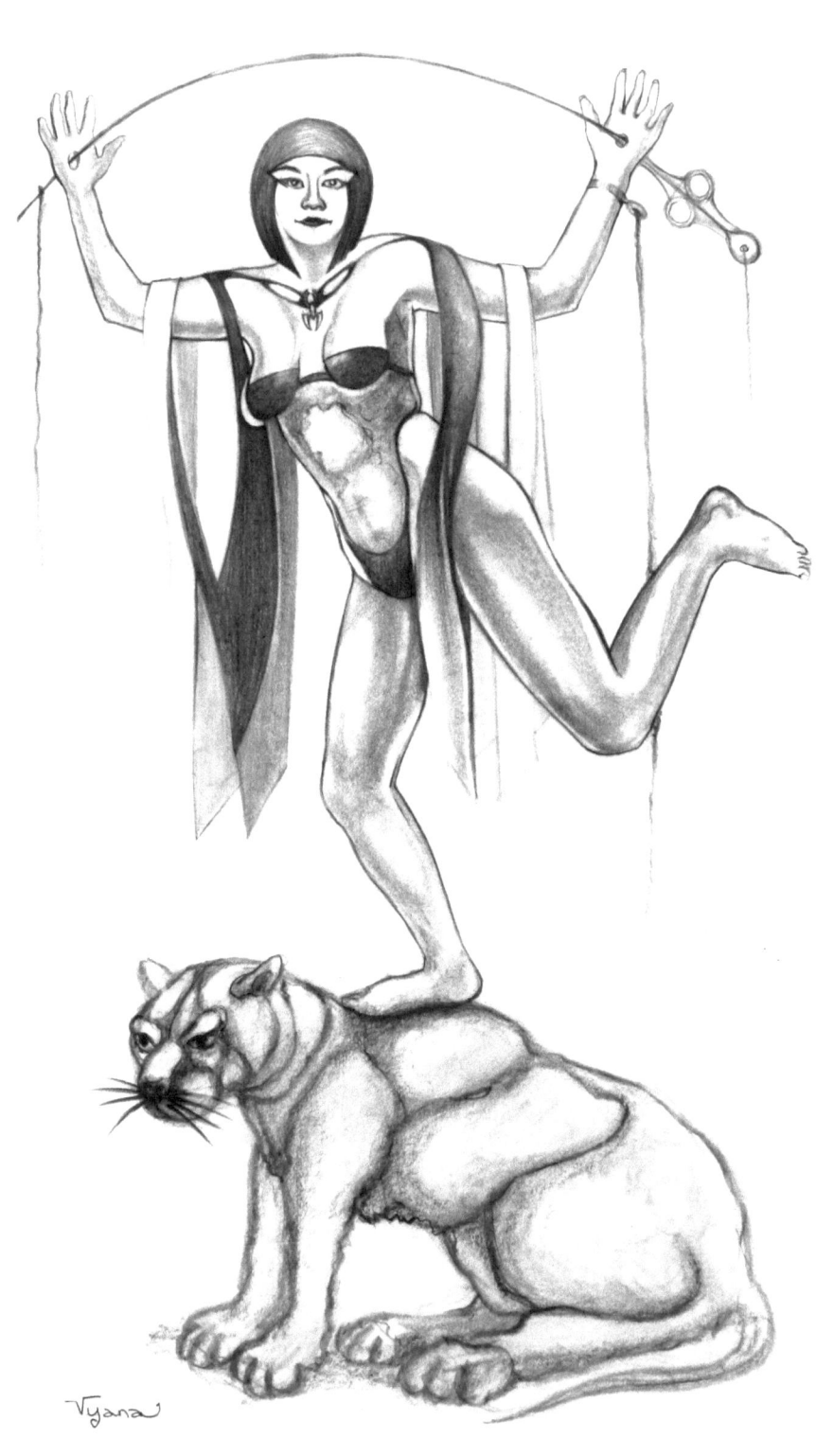

Vyana

Epilogue

thanks to those who were able to grasp something of VALUE hereThere.

i was born into a whirlwind

in a chill air ice-sun November day

No, "I said" this is not for me!!!!!!!!!!!

so, i was born anyways, and did choose not to return to the wOmb.

and, from birthing this "somewhere along the way" poem into life,

and, from the ... IMpossible

i. m. possible

love is ...

Afterword

The Beauty of the Intellect

is that it wonders and discovers.

The Beauty of the Love

is that it never wavers ... love is ...

— vyana

Index of Poems

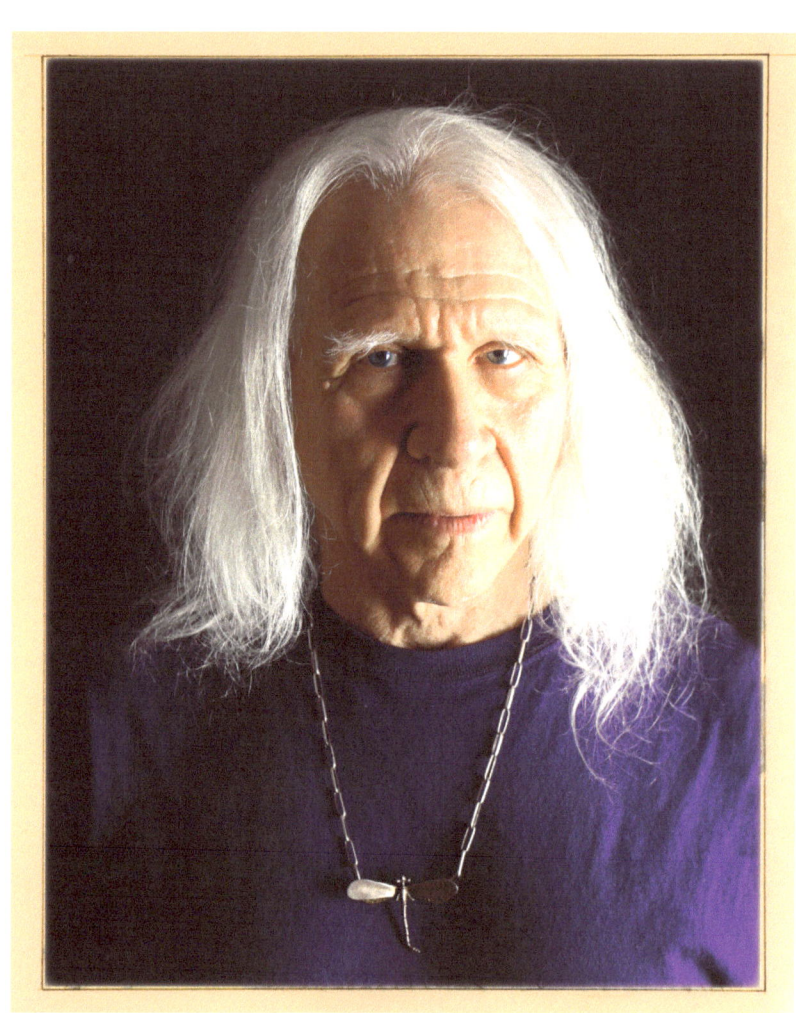

about vyana

poet

artist

sculptor

illustrator

professor

pow wow dancer

loving parent

mentor

and caring friend

DEEPCREATIVITY.ORG

Creativity Consulting

5Phases Consiousness Training

Personal Training

www.ingramcontent.com/pod-product-compliance
Lightning Source LLC
Chambersburg PA
CBHW040755200526
45159CB00026B/2611